HOW TO BUILD YOUR IDEAL

PRACTICE IN 90 DAYS

HOW TO BUILD YOUR IDEAL

PRACTICE IN 90 DAYS

*A Practical Guide To Having More Fun, Clients, Money,
Success, and Fulfillment In Your Private Practice With Less
Time And Money Than You Thought Possible*

DAVID STEELE, M.A.

To order additional copies of this book, contact:
Xlibris Corporation
1-888-795-4274
www.Xlibris.com
Orders@Xlibris.com
17009-STEE

Introduction

Welcome! This book is designed to help coaches, therapists, social workers, chiropractors, and other private practitioners, to design and build your ideal practice in 90 days, with less time and money than you thought possible.

All of the assignments in this program can be completed in just minutes per day, at low or no cost. How much time and money you devote to building your practice is entirely up to you. Sometimes, less is more!

> ➤ **RULE #1 of this program is *FIRST THINGS FIRST*.** I suggest a steady, linear, and disciplined approach to building your practice by scheduling an hour or two per week to focus on this program, which is cumulative and works best when completing the assignments in order over time—at least 90 days. I suggest you put these scheduled times in your calendar and treat them as seriously as a client appointment.

Rushing through the assignments, spending a lot of time trying to get them "perfect," skipping assignments, and doing them out of order is *not* recommended. By plodding forward, completing the assignments in order a little at a time, you will be *amazed* at how much you can accomplish in 90 days!

> ➤ **RULE #2 of this program is *FREE FIRST*.** *The most effective techniques for getting clients don't cost anything!*

Spending money is not a substitute for good business practices, and can sabotage your success. Save your capital for when you are clear that it will be well invested in your business.

I provide many FREE resources for business cards, web sites, auto-responders, and more. *These recommendations alone can save you hundreds, even thousands of dollars,* paying for this book many times over!

> ➢ **Rule #3 of this program is *GET CLIENTS.*** We can get so absorbed in the details of building a practice that we forget to focus upon our main goal, which is to identify and work with our ideal clients. From this moment forward, commit to taking advantage of every opportunity you can find to reach the folks you want to help and invite them to hire you. *Everything else is secondary.*

After many years in private practice, burning up thousands of hours and dollars learning what does and doesn't work by trial and error, I became passionate about helping other practitioners have successful and fulfilling practices.

This program developed organically in my work as a Mentor Coach helping hundreds of private practitioners design and build their ideal practices, and I sincerely hope it will help you to achieve your personal and professional dreams.

Note #1: Please review the "Best Practice Building Tips" section and note short and long-term actions items. Most information you might need to implement the assignments are in this section.

Note #2: You don't have to do this alone! I invite you to join my next 90-Day Practice Building Intensive. For more information visit *http://www.BuildingYourIdealPractice.com*

Note #3: You can go much farther and faster with a coach. I would be pleased and honored to help you design and build your ideal practice. Please contact me at *David@Steele.name* to discuss working together.

Note #4: Don't just passively read through this program— *DO IT!* You will greatly increase your likelihood of success if you get into action and take the trouble to put the assignments in writing. The Universe can't give you what you don't ask for! *If you do what you've always done, you'll get what you've always got.*

Contents

I. Weekly Assignments

Note: Timing of assignments is paced to be completed in 90 days. You can choose to complete them faster or slower than is suggested below.

Week #1: Pages 14-19

Assignment #1: My 3 Month Miracle; where do you want to be in 3 months as a result of this program?

Assignment #2: Where I Am Now; assess the current status of your practice.

Assignment #3: My Ideal Practice; describe your ideal practice in as much detail as possible.

Week #2: Pages 20-27

Assignment #4: My Purpose; what is the purpose of your life, and how do you want to express that purpose in your work?

Assignment #5: My Niches; Identify one or more niches that you have a passion for, that you really want to work with, that fit 100% in your ideal practice.

Assignment #6: My Ideal Client; describe your ideal client for each niche

Assignment #7: My Mission; for each niche, how will you help them? What difference will you make with them?

Week #3: Pages 28-33
Assignment #8: My Pinnacle; what is the pinnacle of your professional career that you want to achieve?

Assignment #9: My Laser Speech; for each of your niches, design a "laser speech" for your ideal client in that niche.

Week #4: Pages 34-39

Assignment #10: My Service Delivery System; what are the various products and services that you will offer your clients, and how can you put them together into an organized system?

Week #5 and 6: Pages 40-43
Assignment #11: Market Research; before going further, learn directly from your target audience who they are and what they want.

Week #7: Pages 44-47
Assignment #12: Mining My Base; launching your new practice by creating and using a database of past and current clients, colleagues, referral sources, etc.

Week #8: Pages 48-51
Assignment #13: Internal Marketing; converting prospects to clients, building long-term relationships with clients, prospects and referral sources.

Week #9: Page 52-53
Assignment #14: Assets And Supports; leveraging your

existing assets and supports to help launch or grow your practice.

Week #10: Pages 54-56

Assignment #15: Budget; developing a budget for marketing and practice development.

Week #11: Pages 57-64
Assignment #16: External Marketing Plan; attracting new potential clients

Week #12+: Implementation, trouble-shooting, celebrating progress, etc.

Post-script To Assignments: Page 65

II. Best Practice Building Tips

III. Appendix

I
ASSIGNMENTS

Assignment #1

MY 3-MONTH MIRACLE

Describe where do you want to be in 3 months as a result of this program. Try to stretch beyond what you might judge to be "realistic," but make it achievable to set yourself up for success. List at least 3 measurable goals that right now would seem like a "miracle" to achieve.

_____

_____

_____

_____

_____

_____

_____

_____

_____

_____

_____

_____

_____

_____

_____

_____

_____

_____

_____

_____

_____

Assignment #2

WHERE I AM NOW

Describe the current status of your practice. Include the following:

a. What are your working days and hours? _____

b. Who are your clients? _____

c. What do you do with your clients? _____

_____

d. What is your income? _____

e. How do your clients find you? _____

_____

f. Why do your clients choose to work with YOU? _____

_____

g. What do you do in addition to working with clients? ____

_____

h. Do you have more than one revenue stream? If so, what?

_____

i. Do you have passive income/activities? If so, what? _____

_____

j. Do you work alone or with others? _____

k. What are you recognized for among your peers and in your community? _____

_____

_____

_____

_____

_____

_____

_____

_____

_____

ASSIGNMENT #3

MY IDEAL PRACTICE

Describe your ideal practice in as much detail as possible. Below are some questions to get you started. Treat your Ideal Practice as a Vision. There is no need to answer the questions literally; they are just to stimulate you. Please include ideas that occur to you about your ideal practice that are not mentioned in the questions.

a. What are your working days and hours?
b. Who are your clients?
c. What are you doing with your clients?
d. What income are you producing?
e. How do your clients find you?
f. Why do your clients choose to work with YOU?
g. What do you do in addition to working with clients?
h. Do you have more than one revenue stream?
i. Do you have passive income/activities?
j. Do you work alone or with others?
k. What are your gifts to your clients and the community?
l. What are you recognized for?
m. Do you publish anything?
n. When you retire, how will the legacy of your gifts live on?

MY IDEAL PRACTICE:

_____
_____
_____
_____
_____
_____
_____
_____

_____

_____

_____

_____

_____

_____

_____

_____

_____

_____

_____

_____

_____

_____

_____

_____

_____

_____

_____

_____

_____

_____

_____

_____

_____

_____

_____

_____

_____

Assignment #4

MY PURPOSE

Looking at your vision of your Ideal Practice, as well as other purpose work you may have completed to date:

- ♦ What seems to be the Purpose of your work?
- ♦ What difference are you trying to make in the world as a helping professional?
- ♦ What is the purpose of your life, and how do you want to express that purpose in your work?

If you think of your Ideal Practice as a city on a map, that you have chosen out of all the possible places in the world to live and work, your purpose is WHAT you want to accomplish in that place.

As an example, the purpose of my life (David) is to *"create a world of love and empowerment by loving and empowering myself and others ."*

My work is how I express the purpose of my life. The purpose of my work is to: *"Improve the quality of life and relationships in my community for children and adults, marriages, and families, by helping singles and couples to have successful Life Partnerships"*

Write a purpose statement for your practice:

_____

_____

_____

_____

_____

_____

_____

_____

ASSIGNMENT #5

MY NICHES

Looking at your Ideal Practice and your Purpose, WHERE are your clients?

If your Ideal Practice were a city on a map, your niches would be the communities in which you would work.

Many communities co-exist in the same location, such as a Christian church on one corner, and a Jewish synagogue on the other. A niche is a group of clients that are in a similar situation.

Identify one or more niches that you have a PASSION for, that you *WANT* to work with, that EXCITE you, that fit 100% in your IDEAL PRACTICE. Be as specific as possible.

Examples:

♦ Pre-committed, two career couples in their 20's and 30's who have never been married
♦ Successful millionaire entrepreneurs who built their business from scratch and are wondering what to do next
♦ Second or third-time single women, age 50+ who want to find their life partner
♦ Engineers who have discovered there is more to life than their work and don't know where to start"

Tip: niches are *NOT "features"* of your prospective client, such as "motivated," "successful," "want to change," etc.

My Niches:

#1:_____

_____

_____
_____
_____
_____
_____

#2:_____
_____
_____
_____
_____

#3:_____
_____
_____
_____
_____

#4:_____
_____
_____
_____
_____

#5:_____
_____
_____
_____
_____
_____
_____

ASSIGNMENT #6

MY IDEAL CLIENT

Describe your ideal client for *EACH niche.*

    If your practice were a city on a map, of all the residents of the city, WHOM would you ask to hire you?

    Be as specific as possible. Describe their lifestyle, work, background, education, interests, leisure preferences, etc.

My Ideal Clients:

Niche #1:_____

_____

_____

_____

_____

_____

Niche #2:_____

_____

_____

_____

_____

Niche #3: _____

_____

_____

_____

_____

Niche #4: _____

_____

_____

_____

_____

_____

_____

Niche #5: _____

_____

_____

_____

_____

_____

_____

_____

_____

_____

_____

_____

_____

_____

_____

_____

_____

_____

_____

_____

_____

_____

_____

_____

_____

_____

_____

_____

_____

_____

ASSIGNMENT #7

MY MISSION

For EACH niche/ideal client, HOW do you want to help them?

Would you help them throw their mother off a train? Probably not. You want to help them in ways aligned with your purpose.

What do they want, that you want to help them achieve, that if you approached your ideal client and asked them to hire you, *GUARANTEEING their success,* they could not refuse?

1. If your Ideal Practice is a city on a map . . .

2. Your Purpose is your reason for being there . . .

3. Your Niche is where you would find your clients . . .

4. Your Ideal Client would be who you want to work with . . .

   and . . .

5. Your Mission would be how you want to help them.

Here is my mission statement for my work with singles: *"To provide the information, tools, and support needed for singles to find the love of their life and the life that they love."*

For couples, it is to*: "Help couples co-create a fulfilling and lasting life partnership of ever deepening trust, love, intimacy, and connection."*

Write a mission statement for EACH niche/ideal client

Niche #1: _____

_____

_____

_____

_____

_____

Niche #2: _____

_____

_____

_____

_____

_____

Niche #3: _____

_____

_____

_____

_____

_____

Niche #4: _____

_____

_____

_____

_____

_____

Niche #5: _____

_____

_____

_____

_____

_____

ASSIGNMENT # 8

MY PINNACLE

For your ideal practice, you created a vision of what you want for your life and work.

For this assignment, please expand on that and vision the PINNACLE of your practice—when you have been having your ideal practice and built your business to the point that you have "arrived," or are ready to retire (or not!) satisfied that you have reached the absolute top of what you want to achieve.

It may be helpful to refer to previous assignments to make sure you include your mission, purpose, niches, etc.

_____
_____
_____
_____
_____
_____
_____
_____
_____
_____
_____
_____
_____
_____
_____
_____
_____
_____
_____

ASSIGNMENT #9

MY LASER SPEECH

For each of your niches, design a "laser speech" for your ideal client in that niche. Envision your ideal client asking, "What do you do?" and design your response to be captivating and compelling TO YOUR IDEAL CLIENT!

A good laser speech is brief, mentions your niche and the main benefit of working with you, and expresses a lot about you as a professional. This helps to qualify your prospects, as your ideal client will be very attracted to what you are saying because it resonates for them, and people that are not interested in your gifts (that you would not really want to work with anyway) will not resonate with what you are saying.

To write your laser speech, review all your previous assignments, and pick out the most compelling words to describe what you do.

As an example, for my niche of working with pre-committed couples, reviewing all that I have written recently, I might say:

> *"Do you know any couples that want to be careful and conscious about entering a committed relationship? I'm a relationship coach, and I empower new couples to be 'at choice' and create conscious, intentional, and sustainable committed life partnerships."*

Now, I don't pretend to be the best model for anyone, but if you look closely at the above laser speech, you will notice a few things:

1. I started with an engaging question. Try it without

the question and it still works . . . this is a preference thing.

2. I asked, "Do you know . . ." . . . . Get the hook?
   This gives them room to answer, "YES—THAT'S
   ME!", or answer, "Yes, I do know someone", or
   answer "No."

Any way they answer, I have valuable info . . . I have either qualified them, found out they are a possible referral
source, or disqualified them—IN THE FIRST 5 SECONDS!

3. I used language that is powerful for me . . . I
   didn't use "help" or "coach," I used "empower,"
   which is a value I have that is represented in my
   mission and purpose statements.

4. I educated the listener about some things that
   may be new to them . . . "new couples," being
   "careful," being "at choice".. this is a mini-semi-
   nar, and invites them to pick up on the concept
   that attracts them and ask me about it.

5. My niche is clearly identified: new couples, who
   want to be careful/intentional/conscious, and
   want a committed life partnership.

Given this laser speech, if a couple isn't new, they wish
to stay unconscious, and they don't value commitment, then
they clearly would not fit for me.

6. By saying "conscious," "intentional," and "at
   choice," I am specifying that I wish to work with
   couples that wish to honor themselves and be
   open to unchoosing the relationship if necessary

to laying the foundation for their future relationship success.

I don't wish to work with desperate, unconscious couples that want to "make" their relationship work and force the round peg in the square hole.

This is concisely expressed and will resonate with folks I want to work with, and will probably scare off the folks that I don't wish to work with!

Write a laser speech for EACH niche/ideal client

Niche #1:_____

_____

_____

_____

_____

_____

Niche #2:_____

_____

_____

_____

_____

Niche #3: _____

_____

_____

_____

_____

Niche #4: _____

_____

_____

Niche #5:

ASSIGNMENT #10

MY SERVICE DELIVERY SYSTEM

You are a talented helping professional with a clear vision of your ideal practice, well-defined purpose and mission, serving defined niches, seeking your ideal clients in each niche.

Before we proceed to marketing and getting clients, first you must decide if your services will be to disconnected niches, or if you can string them together into a service delivery system.

A system allows clients to enter your practice at multiple points, and any marketing activity can be maximized to support your other niches.

For example, I am a "full service" relationship coach, and I serve singles, uncommitted and committed couples. I have interest and expertise in parenting, family businesses, workplace relationships, stepfamilies, mediation, etc.

When I market to anyone anywhere in the relationship continuum, they:

(A) Are likely to have related needs other than the obvious one I am marketing
(B) Are likely to have future needs I can help with,
(C) Are likely to know someone that has needs I can help with

Being clear about the "pipeline" for my practice (singles become couples, couples become parents, etc) allows me to integrate my marketing. For example, at my events for singles, everyone that attends is educated about our readiness class, attraction coaching teams, and programs for new couples.

By being clear about your service delivery system, you can design your marketing to communicate how you can help your prospective clients, you can plant the seed that you can help them when they reach the next step as well, and you can stimulate word of mouth by inviting them to share with people that they care about.

> This is a critical activity. Even if you think your niches are disparate and have nothing in common, you may get a brainstorm that helps you bring the pieces together. Try talking to friends and colleagues about this, and they may spark an idea for you.

Look at your niches and see if you can identify a common thread that you can string together and create a *"Service Delivery System."*

1. List the services you offer people
Mine are:
♦ Mentor Coaching
♦ Practice Development Coaching
♦ Teaching/training relationship coaching
♦ Relationship Coaching

2. List who you offer your services to
Mine are:
♦ Coaches
♦ Therapists
♦ Singles
♦ Couples

3. List how you deliver your services
Mine are:
♦ telephone
♦ teleclass
♦ in person

- group
- individual
- on line

4. Combine the above as you want to practice
Mine are:

- Mentor Coaching for coaches and therapists over the telephone and in teleclasses, individually and in groups
- Teaching relationship coaching and training helping professionals in relationship coaching in teleclasses
- Relationship coaching for singles, in person or over the telephone, individually or in groups/classes
- Relationship coaching for couples, in person or over the telephone

5. Identify areas of possible overlap
Mine are:

- My mentees could be single or couples and need relationship coaching, or be interested in learning relationship coaching
- My students or trainees could be single or couples and need relationship coaching, they also might want me to mentor coach them
- My singles might become couples
- My couples might become single again

6. What new possibilities does the above bring up for you?

- I could be more aggressive with my students/trainees about my availability as a mentor coach
- I could offer relationship coaching to my mentees and students

◆ I should let my singles know about my coaching program for new couples
◆ I should follow up with couples that don't make it and offer singles coaching

7. Tie all the above together in a Service Delivery System.

How will you create a system where your clients learn about your other services in a way that supports them to take advantage of what you offer?

For example, I could:
◆ Offer my single clients a discount for returning when they are in a pre-committed relationship
◆ Create a newsletter for my singles, and another for couples, and market the couples services and newsletter to the singles.
◆ Create a coaching team for single helping professionals

➢ **Be creative about what you offer and how you can integrate your services so each service/niche can potentially feed the other.**

➢ **It is much more effective to offer a continuum of services to your existing clients, than to always need new blood, so go for it!**

Some questions to consider in designing your Service Delivery System:

1. What are the common needs of the clients in your niches?

2. What interventions do you find yourself using over and over?

3. If you were to write ONE newsletter for your practice, what would you call it and whom would you send it to?

4. Is there someone in your field that you can emulate, learn from, and provide a model to draw from?

5. If you were to give your practice a name (fictitious business name), what might that be?

NOTES ON MY SERVICE DELIVERY SYSTEM:

_____

_____

_____

_____

_____

_____

_____

_____

_____

_____

_____

_____

_____

_____

_____

_____

_____

_____

_____

_____

_____

_____

_____

_____

_____

_____

_____

_____

_____

_____

_____

_____

_____

_____

_____

_____

_____

_____

_____

_____

> **Are you clear on your ideal practice, niches, ideal clients, laser speeches, and service delivery?**

" If so . . . congratulations! You are on your way!

" If not . . . please get the support that you need.

ASSIGNMENT # 11

MARKET RESEARCH

This next assignment is critical and often overlooked. This should be fun for you once you start, but will most likely take at least a couple of weeks.

THIS IS PROBABLY THE MOST IMPORTANT AS-SIGNMENT OF THIS PROGRAM. By itself, *THIS CAN LAUNCH YOUR PRACTICE!*

To my knowledge, everyone that has done all the steps of this next assignment has *gotten at least one client from it!* How is that for incentive?

So far, you have been going inside to be clear about what you want to do and how you want to do it. *Now is the time to learn from your target audience who they are and what they want.*

1. For *each* of your niches, find two or three people that fit your ideal client profile and interview them.

Pretty brazen, huh? Well, this is the kind of "putting yourself out there" that makes for a successful private practice. As an alternative to individual interviews, you could pull together a focus group (could be over the telephone). Offer them something (tape, free session, free admission to an event you host, etc) for their participation.

> A. Tell them why you identified them as resembling your ideal client. See how close to the mark you were in pegging them as fitting your ideal client profile. If you were way off, try to note ideas for how to choose better.

B. Try out your laser speech and ask for their feedback about what turns them on and what doesn't.

C. Describe how you help your clients and ask for
their reaction. Are they attracted? To what? What
are they not attracted to?

D. Describe your service delivery system and ask for
their feedback. Would it meet their needs? What
needs do they have that you have not addressed?
What suggestions do they have?

E. Show them your business card, fliers, web site,
brochure, etc and get their feedback. Find out
what would be compelling and get their attention. Show them what you have, don't put this off
until everything is in place. Ideally, your market
research will be an on-going process.

F. Ask them what they read/subscribe to (for advertising, press releases, submitting articles), where
they hang out/shop/work out/go for entertain-
ment (for marketing venues), what professional
services they use (accountant, lawyer, massage
therapist, etc) and for their contact information
(for cross referrals).

G. ASK FOR THE REFERRAL! Ask if they know
anyone who would benefit from your services and
give them your card, flyer, etc. (they just might
refer themselves!)

CAUTION: Most professionals that do this end up with at
least one interviewee wanting to hire them, so BE PRE-
PARED FOR SUCCESS!

2. For each of your niches, survey "the competition."

Who else is serving your target audience and how? Contact at least two and interview them about their business; most are happy to talk about what they do. Be mindful of possibilities for collaboration. Be open for inspirations about how to improve upon, or differentiate yourself from, what they are doing.

3. Compile your data:

A. What to continue doing
B. What to stop doing
C. What to do differently
D. Marketing venues (places to develop relationships with, promote to their participants)
E. PR venues (TV, radio, newspaper, magazines, etc)
F. Allied professionals and businesses for cross-promotion, referrals
G. Like-minded colleagues for collaboration
H. Anything else that comes up for you about your target audience, competition, and context *FOR EACH NICHE!*

_____

_____

_____

_____

_____

_____

_____

_____

_____

ASSIGNMENT #12

MINING MY BASE

When you are ready to roll out your new practice, the best and easiest place to start is with people you already know. *It is far more effective to market to your existing leads, than to generate new leads,* which is the theme of the next two assignments.

You have many people that already know you and may be interested in your new practice, for themselves or someone they know.

THIS ASSIGNMENT IS CRITICAL—DO NOT SKIP IT! Your future marketing efforts depend upon having your database in place.

Step 1: Obtain database software

♦ Option A: You can learn to use the programs bundled with your computer, such as Microsoft Excel, Outlook, or Access.

♦ Option B: Buy a software program that fits your needs. I would suggest a contact management software such as ACT! 2000 (*http://www.act.com/*) that not only keeps your database, but helps you track your relationship with each prospect or client.

Do an internet search for the best price. I recommend going to www.ebay.com and searching for ACT! 2000, which can be found for under $20.00. Never tried E-Bay? I have had good experiences so far with them.

♦ Option C: For on-line database services, you can

create a Yahoo Groups site for that purpose along with your newsletter list at *www.yahoogroups.com,* or *www.quickbase.com,* which is free when your use is small, then upgrade as needed.

Step 2: Compile a database of everyone you know

♦ Friends
♦ Family
♦ Neighbors
♦ Church acquaintances
♦ Former colleagues
♦ Former co-workers
♦ College friends
♦ Former clients
♦ Former prospective clients
♦ Friends of friends
♦ Friends of friends of friends of friends

Gather names, telephone numbers, e-mail addresses from every source you have. Look through old files, collections of business cards, and address books. While you are at it, resolve to get the contact info of EVERY person you talk to about your business in the future and add them to this list.

Step 3: Input the folks from Step 2 into your database

Step 4: Plan an introductory event to roll out your new practice

♦ Teleclass
♦ Open house
♦ Seminar/presentation
♦ Premiums (book, tape, free service, etc)

Step 5: Send a letter (snail mail preferred for the first time, then follow up with e-mail) announcing your new practice and inviting them to participate in your introductory event. ASK THEM TO "PLEASE SHARE WITH SOMEONE YOU CARE ABOUT"!

It is best to make this mailing very professional looking . . . an embossed invitation, a 3-color brochure, etc. It is best to have your picture and logo prominently displayed (don't have one? Get one!)

Step 6: Implement!

_____

_____

_____

_____

_____

_____

_____

_____

_____

_____

_____

_____

_____

_____

_____

_____

_____

Assignment #13

INTERNAL MARKETING

"External Marketing" is the process of generating new leads. "*Internal Marketing*" is the process of building a relationship with your existing leads, with the goal of being hired or referred to. *80% of sales are made with 5 or more contacts.*

Once you have your database set up, your goal is to add to it and have an effective, on-going internal marketing program. We will look at external marketing later, but it is far more important for you to take care of the leads you already have, than to add more leads.

Step 1: Plan how to keep in touch

- Newsletter (how often?)
- Announcements
- Seasonal contacts (Valentine's day, Christmas, etc)
- Check ins (telephone or e-mail)
- Contests
- "R & D Team"
- Etc

Step 2: Plan your "gifts"; tangibles for contacting you, showing up, referring a friend, etc

- Complimentary service
- Free tape or book
- Article or white paper
- Handout
- Checklist
- E-book
- E-Program

- "Membership"
- Mentioning in your newsletter
- Listserv community
- "Member" events
- Etc

Step 3: Infuse your marketing into your collateral materials, web site, e-mails, etc. Here are some ideas:

- Your e-mail address needs to market for you; *Jim@GreatRelationships.com* works *barb123@aol.com* DOES NOT WORK FOR YOU!

- Your e-mail signature needs to market for you; subscribe invitation to your newsletter, respond for free tape, etc. Include your web site, e-mail address, telephone #, business name, mission statement

- Your business card should have your mission statement on it, a graphic and or picture. Even better is to have a "Top 5" tips list on the back

- Your brochure should have an insert or tear-off response card with checklist of interests for follow up.

- Your web site should have lots of calls to action; free tape or article, e-program, subscribe to newsletter, contest, questionnaire, self-test, "Ask The Coach," etc

- Every presentation, teleclass, etc should start by getting contact info from participants, and end by asking participants for feedback, including questions about what they want more information about, and a check box giving you permission to contact them.

♦ *Think of at least 5 more for your unique practice!* If you need ideas, see "Best Practice Building Tips" section below.

Step 4: Plan how to "close"

♦ Once a prospect has expressed interest, how will you follow up with them?

♦ Once you follow up with them, how will you get the appointment or sale?

Write this down and practice it. Get ideas and support for closing effectively. See *Converting Prospects To Customers* in "Best Practice Building Tips."

Since most helping professionals are terrible at sales, it may be worth your while to consider hiring a "Closer"—a salesperson who will follow up your leads and close the sale for you. Ideally, this would be somebody who is enthusiastic about what you do and will work part time on commission. Don't be so fast to rule this out! Think about it; would you rather have 100% of 5 clients/participants, or 80% of 15 clients/participants? Do the math!

_____

_____

_____

_____

_____

_____

_____

ASSIGNMENT #14

ASSETS AND SUPPORTS

In this assignment we will look at how to leverage your existing assets and supports to help launch or grow your practice.

1. *Networking Connections*—go through your database and separate out those people that have a useful connection for you with other professionals, groups, organizations that your target audience belongs, etc. For each person, ask yourself "Who do they know that would be helpful to me?" List each person along with the connections they have.

ACTION PLAN: Plan to connect with them by taking them to lunch (or similar) and engaging their support.

2. *Champions*—go through your database and identify people that think you are great, that have the personality and ability to talk you up to others, and have most likely already made referrals to you.

ACTION PLAN: Plan to take them to lunch (or similar) and engaging their support. You may consider "comping" (complimentary admission to your class, free coaching for a month, etc) as a way to encourage and reinforce them.

3. *Trainings, credentials, past employment experience, etc.*

ACTION PLAN: See how you can use them to help you in your present work. What are the commonalities between what you did and what you are doing now? How can you use what you did in the past to support what you are doing now?

4. *Communities*—groups that you belong to, have belonged to, or could join, that could support your present goals.

ACTION PLAN: strategize how to connect with them, give back to them, contribute to them, and ask for support from them

_____

_____

_____

_____

_____

_____

_____

_____

_____

_____

_____

_____

_____

_____

_____

_____

_____

_____

_____

_____

_____

ASSIGNMENT #15

BUDGET

Your goal is to build a business that will have a long, successful life. Any time, effort, and money spent, is an investment in your future.

1. *RISK TOLERANCE*—what level of risk can you live with? If you are the sole support of your family, your risk tolerance might be very low, if you are independently wealthy with no heirs, your level of risk tolerance might be very high. Rate your level of risk tolerance on a scale from 0 (low) to 10 (high)

2. *NET WORTH*—add your assets and subtract your liabilities

3. *AVAILABLE CREDIT*—add up the credit available to you from your home equity, credit cards, etc.

4. *LIQUID ASSETS*—how much cash (or near cash assets) to you have easy access to?

5. *RESERVES*—Do you have at 3 months living expenses on hand? Can you survive negative cash flow for a year?

6. *Considering your risk tolerance, assets, credit, and reserve needs, what is the maximum amount you can consider budgeting for your building your Ideal Practice?*

You may not need much start-up capital or need to go

into more debt, but it is useful to know how much you could use if you wanted. You could choose to build slowly, as time and money is available, or transition quickly by quitting your job, or somewhere in between. Your choice will depend upon your answers to the above questions.

7. **CREATE BUDGET**—list the main categories (marketing, rent, supplies, postage, etc.) that your practice will need, and allocate percentages (not dollar amounts) for each. Apply the percentages to #6 above and that is your "quick and dirty" tentative budget!

8. PLAN CASH FLOW-

A. Estimate the "case size" of each client (how much a client, on average will pay you in a year). For fun, you can go back to last year, add the total # of clients you served, divide by your gross income, and that will be the "case size" of your previous practice.

B. Estimate how much you would make for each month in the coming year, being conservative about the # of new clients coming into your practice each month, using "case size" divided by 12 to figure your monthly income.

C. Based upon your budget (#7) and your estimates above, figure your P + L (profit and loss) for each month in the next year, and from there estimate how much of your budget you can spend to build your practice each month. When you complete your business/marketing plan, this will be how much you will plan to spend on it.

Assignment #16

EXTERNAL MARKETING PLAN

The final assignment of *How To Build Your Ideal Practice In 90 Days* is designing your external marketing plan, which is how you will reach the public to generate new leads for your practice.

This assignment is last because:

♦ External marketing is costly

♦ It tends to be much less effective than internal marketing

♦ To be effective, must be part of a *SYSTEMATIC* BUSINESS/MARKETING PLAN, and not done in isolation.

STEP 1: Review all of your previous assignments and make sure they are thoroughly completed before continuing.

STEP 2: Determine your budget for external marketing for your first year, AFTER necessary expenses such as setting up your web site, designing and printing your collateral materials (logo, business cards, stationary, envelopes, brochures, flyers, etc).

STEP 3: Plan your low cost alternatives first. For each one that you choose, plan how to integrate it into your system, going so far as to mark your calendar a year in advance when you will take these actions.

EXTERNAL MARKETING OPTIONS:

A. PRESS RELEASES; get the contact info of the news publications most likely to be read by your ideal clients and plan to send them regular press releases prior to your events, seasonally relevant times (Valentine's Day, Christmas, etc), in response to current events, etc. Be sure to write it as if a reporter wrote it, and include an interesting photo, and they may print it as is!

➤ NEWSPAPERS WANT NEWS AND WANT TO HEAR FROM YOU!

Having a news article about you will establish you as THE expert in your niche in your community, and will lead to ubiquitous opportunities that you couldn't possibly predict (or buy!), even if you wrote it yourself!

B. SUBMIT ARTICLES; get the contact info of magazines and other publications (e-zines, human interest section of the newspaper, shoppers weekly, etc) most likely to be read by your ideal clients that accept and print articles. When one of yours gets printed, take that as a sign that they like your material, and approach them about writing a regular column.

➤ PUBLICATIONS WANT CONTENT—GIVE THEM YOURS!

C. CO-BRAND; identify complementary businesses that serve your ideal clients and offer to collaborate. This could be cross-referral, cross-promotion, or even co-sponsoring events and services together.

➤ BUSINESSES ALWAYS WANT WAYS TO INCREASE THEIR BUSINESS—SHOW THEM HOW WORKING WITH YOU WILL DO THAT!

D. LETTERS TO THE EDITOR; in response to current events in the news that relate to your niche, write regular letters to the editor providing your input. Your potential clients will read them, and well as media sources that may contact you as an expert.

➤ THE PUBLIC NEEDS THE NEWS BALANCED WITH INFORMED OPINIONS AND FACTS THAT REPORTERS OMIT—GIVE THEM YOURS!

E. RADIO/TELEVISION; record yourself giving a presentation, or prepare a sample of your content and style in an audition tape and send it to your local radio and/or television station.

➤ THE MEDIA IS ALWAYS LOOKING FOR FRESHNESS— YOU COULD BE THEIR NEXT DARLING!

F. ANNOUNCEMENTS; gather the contact information of all the publications and sections (there may be more than one) of the newspaper that run free announcements, and plan to submit regular announcements regarding your presentations and seminars. Sometimes publications will only accept announcements of non-profit organizations; go ahead and submit anyway. Once they see that your program is helping others they probably will not question your tax status.

G. NETWORKING; continually build your referral network and cross-referral relationships by contacting new businesses or professionals. Commit to contacting two or more new possibilities per week. Find them in advertisements, yellow pages, etc. Call them to ask about their business, and in the process share about yours. Offer to drop by for a visit or to go for coffee.

➢ WHEN YOU CONTACT OTHER BUSINESSES AND PROFESSIONALS INTERESTED IN WHAT THEY DO, YOU WILL USUALLY BE VERY WELL RECEIVED.

STEP 4: ADVERTISING; For most helping professionals, this is the least effective means of getting clients. The responses that you do get often are not very well qualified (meaning they are not anywhere close to your ideal clients!), and will be calling for "information" and to ask "how much?"

On the other hand, when you are starting a practice and have a budget to do so, advertising can pay off.

1. **Decide what to advertise**. Specific tangibles are better than abstract intangibles. Advertising "Make A Million Dollars In 5 Easy Steps" will work better than "Get Rich Quick." "6 week Partners In Life Program For Couples" is better than "Pre-Marital Counseling." One-day public seminars are better than open-ended services.

2. **Include a compelling reason to contact you, also known as a "Call to Action."** This could be a

special offer such as a discount for early callers, "free tape," a "top ten" list, etc. Be wary of using "Free initial consultation" which only works when they have already decided to try you, or want something for free. Decide upon an attractive, safe, earlier step to take to contact you. See *Get Results With A Call To Action* in "Best Practice Building Tips."

3. **Include your web site and/or e-mail address.** Prospects often feel safer contacting you indirectly at first.

4. **Plan to "test" your advertising.** Do not lock your self into a long-term contract at first. Design a few attractive ads, decide which publications to place them and where, and test the response rate for 1-4 weeks before going further.

5. **Display ads are better than classified,** but cost more up front. It is more costly to place a cheap ad that gets poor response, than to place an expensive ad that pays off for you.

6. **TRACK-TRACK-TRACK-TRACK-TRACK!** (Get the picture?) Tracking the responses to your ads is critical! Advertising is expensive and you can only make good decisions if you know the results.

Create a tracking form for each ad, including categories such as *Publication, Date, Name* (of respondee), *Appointment* (did they make an appointment with you?), *Reason For Calling, Income* (you can track actual income or use your "case size," which you can get by adding up your gross income and dividing by # of clients seen). *See Appendix for a sample "Client Tracking Form."*

Collect the above data, divide the cost of the ad by the income it generated and you have your "*Return On Investment*" (ROI). For example, a $600.00 ad that generated $1,800.00 in income gives you an ROI of .33 or 3 to 1; you made $3.00 for every $1.00 that you spent, which is not bad!

7. **Advertise in the Yellow Pages of the telephone book** *ONLY IF YOUR IDEAL CLIENT IS LIKELY TO FIND YOU THERE!* The yellow pages works very well for some services, and not at all for others. Look carefully at the other ads in the section you are considering, call some and ask how it works for them, and if you decide to proceed, have your ad professionally prepared in a way that helps you stand out from the others to your ideal clients. This can be very expensive and, even more so if you cut corners and don't get the ROI you need to justify the ad. Remember that you will be locked in for an entire year!

8. **Signage**; if your office is visible to the public, consider raising your profile with signage, which works 24/7 and is usually a one-time cost.

9. **Internet Advertising**; There are many web sites and search engines that will be happy to take your advertising dollars, and the chances of having a decent ROI is small enough to be inadvisable; the over-promising and under-delivering of e-commerce and internet advertising are well known. There are enough co-branding, link and banner exchanges, and affiliate opportunities out there that don't cost anything up front, that paying for

internet advertising doesn't seem necessary or prudent. Do you really expect your ideal clients to find you this way?

STEP 5: CREATE A TIME LINE; your goal is to pull together the results of the previous assignments and create a step marketing "system" integrated with your practice activities and services. Create a time line of your marketing activities, such as presentations, and plan your internal and external marketing to support those activities. Be specific with dates and action plans on your time line. If you do this well, you can make all these decisions once, and simply follow your plan year after year with a few minor adjustments. **See appendix for "Practice Building Planning Calendar."**

_____

_____

_____

_____

_____

_____

_____

_____

_____

_____

_____

_____

_____

_____

_____

_____

_____

_____

_____

_____

Post-script To Assignments

If you are reading this and have completed all of the above assignments—*CONGRATULATIONS!* You are well on your way to building your ideal practice, and among the elite few committed to the discipline and risks necessary to practice right livelihood and make your dreams reality. You WILL succeed.

If you are reading this and have not completed all the assignments, are feeling stuck, overwhelmed and scared, DON'T DESPAIR! Hire a coach to *get the support you need.* With effective support, you can go much *farther, faster,* than you can alone. Review "About The Author" in the appendix and consider contacting me, or use a coach referral service such as www.coachvillereferral.com

I sincerely thank you for purchasing this book and hope it has been helpful to you. Please drop me a line and let me know if you have any feedback, suggestions, and/or wins to share.

Best wishes in your journey to have the life, business, and relationships you really want. I look forward to hearing from you!

Best regards,

David Steele

II
Best Practice
Building Tips

Seven Habits of Highly Successful Private Practicioners

A small percentage of helping professionals are able to reach their financial goals with full time private practice. Most practitioners struggle to make it by working with managed care, accepting part time employment, working for discounted fees, etc.

In my experience mentoring professionals to build their practices, I have found highly successful practitioners to share the following characteristics:

1. PASSIONATE

Highly successful professionals love their work, and are so excited by it that they would do it for free, and have no thought or intention of retirement. They truly could not imagine doing anything else, and consider themselves lucky to have the best job in the world. Their passion is easily expressed, and very attractive to their potential clients.

2. POSITIVE

These professionals always have a 'can do' attitude. They truly believe in themselves and trust that they will find a way around obstacles to survive and thrive, and thus are able to effectively empower their clients to be positive as well. They assume abundance instead of scarcity. While they may experience fears and doubts, they are never reasons for 'no.'

3. ENTREPRENEURIAL

Highly successful professionals have an entrepreneurial attitude, consider their practice a business, and take the trouble to learn and apply the business skills needed to be successful. While most helping professionals understandably wish to focus on serving their clients and resist the business and marketing aspects of their practice, successful professionals enjoy the challenge of pioneering a successful business that is an expression of their gifts, mission, and purpose.

4. PLAY LARGE

Successful professionals are always expanding by growing themselves and their practices. They desire to play as large as they can, and take every opportunity to do so. They get impatient with the status quo, and are always in motion seeking to maximize their time, energy, opportunities, and resources.

5. CREATIVE

Highly successful professionals pioneer their work with their clients and their practice. They like to build on what they've learned, and are excited by developing their own approaches to their work that express their gifts, talents, and perspectives. Most enjoy the thought of writing a book or developing a program that would make a unique and powerful contribution to the world.

6. SERVICE-ORIENTED

Highly successful professionals truly wish to make a difference in the world, and are grateful for the opportunity to be of service to their clients. While they may have their financial goals, they wish to practice 'right-livelihood,' and it is more important for them to fulfill their mission and purpose than it is to be financially successful.

7. WALK THE TALK

Highly successful professionals believe in the value of their work and are enthusiastic clients as well. They put time and effort into developing themselves and building the life that they really want, while they are making a living helping others do so. They have walked in their clients' shoes, and continue to do so.

Building a Business vs. Maintaining a Practice

Most helping professionals in private practice have a goal of having a successful practice, where their services are in demand, they are paid well, and there is a steady stream of clients to fill their calendar. This was my dream for many years!

Achieving this successful practice takes much time, effort, and skill in marketing. Most practitioners seem averse to marketing; hence, most practitioners are not successful. *We want to serve our clients, not sell ourselves.*

To survive, many of us take part time jobs, get on managed care panels, discount our fees, serve populations outside of our areas of interest, etc. There are many workshops for helping professionals who want to 'break free of managed care' by building a 'private pay' practice. This seems a step in the right direction, or is it?

After many years of chasing my dream of having a successful practice, and witnessing countless other helping professionals doing the same, and being unfulfilled in the process, I started re-evaluating the whole system.

It did not seem fair that we dedicate ourselves to improving the lives of others, study and train for years, scrape to get by, and do not get the support and appreciation we deserve from the society we are dedicating ourselves to serving. Why are we so undervalued, when the need for our services is so great? What's wrong with this picture?

Well, we humans have a talent for adaptation, so I saw that I needed to adapt to the system around me. *If an inter-*

vention isn't working, is it the fault of the patient? I decided to stop faulting society for making private practice such an ordeal, and re-think the idea of private practice. It occurred to me that if I wanted to be successful, I needed to 'play large' and greatly expand how I reach my clients and how I serve them. I decided to transition from being a couples therapist to being a relationship coach by building a relationship coaching 'business' in my area, instead of narrowing my goal to building and maintaining a 'practice'.

What is the difference between 'building a business' and 'maintaining a practice'?
Here are a few that occur to me:

MAINTAINING A PRACTICE:

(1) *Exchanging time for dollars*
This is limiting, as we have a finite amount of time available

(2) *Internal focus*
Working only with the clients in your practice, in your office

(3) *Client-centered service*
Focusing on the needs of the client in your office

(4) *Marketing goal is to fill your calendar*
Once the calendar is filled, marketing ceases, or serves to fill your future calendar pages

BUILDING A BUSINESS:

(1) *Creating a system to 'make money while you sleep'*
Unlike exchanging time for dollars, when you

have a business your goal is to build it so that it generates income for you while you are away from it. This requires leveraging your time, creating systems, and 'working ON your business instead of IN your business' (concepts from *'The E-Myth : Why Most Businesses Don't Work and What to Do About It'* by Michael Gerber)

(2) External focus
I have found that building a relationship coaching 'business' requires me to look far beyond the clients in my practice, to establishing collaborations with other practitioners, partnerships with similar and complementary organizations, 'business to business' kinds of activities in addition to serving clients in my practice

(3) Community-centered service
My goal is to be THE relationship coaching resource for my entire community, so I needed to assess the needs of the singles and couples in my area and decide how best to meet those needs.

This required thinking outside of the box of my ideas about what people need and what 'should' work, to really listening to what they say they want, pioneering alternatives that I have not considered before and have not seen elsewhere in my community.

This also meant 'playing large' and assuming a leadership position in my community, which is contrary to the mindset of most practitioners, and certainly was scary for me at first.

(4) Marketing goal is to build your business
Given the above, my marketing goal is to reach

the public, colleagues, and like-minded organizations, to fuel the machine I wanted to create to serve my community from an organizational model rather than one-on-one.

The result of my desire to create a relationship coaching 'business' is apparent today in LifePartnerQuest-Silicon Valley, an organization that sponsors weekly singles events, conducts classes, provides individual and group coaching, and serves couples, mostly without me being directly involved at all, which frees me up to write this article, promote relationship coaching worldwide, and help other practitioners have successful practices, which are my passions.

. . . Which perspective do you prefer?

If your goal is to build a business, how can you . . . .

➤ Play large and serve the most people possible?
➤ Discover what your target clients want and need?
➤ Differentiate yourself, and even own your niche? and . . .
➤ Provide products and services that do not depend upon exchanging your time for dollars?

Five Steps to Launching a New Practice

If you are transitioning from one form of practice to another, or adding a new service/niche to your existing practice, I offer the following 5 steps to leveraging past and current contacts to launch your new practice:

STEP 1: COMPILE CONTACT INFORMATION OF EVERY ONE YOU KNOW:

> Friends
> Family
> Neighbors
> Church acquaintances
> Former colleagues
> Former co-workers
> College friends
> Current clients
> Former clients
> Former prospective clients
> Friends of friends
> Friends of friends of friends of friends

Gather names, telephone numbers, e-mail addresses from every source you have. Look through old files, collections of business cards, and address books.

While you are at it, *resolve to get the contact info of EVERY person you talk to about your business in the future and add them to this list.* Your goal is to build your contact list to a magical critical mass (somewhere between 2000 and 5000) that will result in a full practice with little effort on your part.

STEP 2: INPUT DATA FROM STEP 1 INTO DATABASE

Preferably a contact management system such as *ACT!* (learn how to use it!)

STEP 3: PLAN AN INTRODUCTORY EVENT TO ROLL OUT YOUR NEW PRACTICE:

> Teleclass
> Open house
> Seminar/presentation
> Premiums (book, tape, free service, assessment, etc)

STEP 4: SEND ANNOUNCEMENT:

Send out press releases to the media (yes, this is news!)
Send a professional looking invitation and brochure (w/your picture) to your database in Step 2, and ask them to 'PLEASE SHARE WITH SOMEONE YOU CARE ABOUT'

STEP 5: FOLLOW UP:

Build your relationship with your database via e-mail newsletter or regular announcements, as well as telephone calls with folks that respond to your mailings. *80% of sales are made with 5 or more contacts,* so plan how to keep your name in front of your prospects often enough for them to get around to hiring you.

How To 'Package' Yourself for Success

I notice that most highly successful helping professionals have 'packaged' their services in various ways to create effective marketing and revenue streams.

Examples include:

1. Publishing a book, e-book, or workbook/manual
2. Offering workshops
3. Teaching classes
4. Creating a self-assessment tool
5. Giving presentations
6. Writing a column
7. Publishing a newsletter
8. Designing a self help program
9. Using a name and/or logo for differentiation/branding
10. Producing related events to attract clients

'Packaging' is a powerful way to make your services tangible to your prospective clients (see *10 Ways To Make Your Services Tangible*).

Some forms of packaging, such as writing a book, creating a workshop or class, producing related events, etc, can do much more than exchange your time for dollars. Packaging can generate significant sources of income independent of direct services and your physical presence, allowing you to put your knowledge and creativity to work for you; 'making money while you sleep'.

The thought of creating a package or product can be intimidating, but I have found doing so to be quite natural and organic.

Here are some steps to get started:

(1) Do your practice development homework
You should have your niche well defined and have solid experience.

(2) Identify what is compelling to your target audience
What do they really want/need? What turns them on? What causes them to take action and enroll?

(3) What do you see others doing that attracts you?
Look around at other helping professionals and get ideas from the ones that you would like to emulate.

(4) Record yourself working with your clients
What questions do you ask, interventions do you use, unique concepts/tools/language do you find yourself creating for your niche? Use a tape recorder or write these down over time.

(5) Review the results of the above four steps and review the 10 examples above
What jumps out at you as the place to start? It may be to start branding yourself as the 'Dating Coach For Nerds', or to sponsor singles events, or start writing a column that you can develop into a book. Go with your strength and preference;

writing, public speaking and sponsoring events all draw on different strengths.

(6) Research the alternatives and your market
What and who else is out there? Decide on an approach that is exciting to you and fresh for your target audience.

(7) Get started! Use bite-sized pieces
Don't make the mistake of trying to cover/ include too much. Break your product up into easily covered steps and consider creating a series of products.

(8) Test market
Start with people you know in your niche (friends, colleagues, family, former clients) and ask them to participate at no charge in exchange for giving you experience and feedback.

(9) Refine
There is a lot of 'noise' out there, so work to find effective language for your titles and concepts, make sure your book/newsletter/class/workshop is well organized, clear, fresh, and compelling to your target audience. Test various versions to find the most effective one that will differentiate your product from the others.

(10) Collaborate
Find like-minded colleagues to play with and support each other for mutual benefit, teach other professionals so they and their clients can benefit from your work. Few are successful alone.

(11) Celebrate!

You have given a gift to the world! By creating a product you have taken your knowledge, experience and creativity, and created a legacy that can continue your work beyond your lifetime.

Basic Brochure Design

When designing your practice it is a useful exercise to design a dummy brochure, or several. Whether you will actually use a brochure or not, the process involved in creating one often brings your Service Delivery System, marketing and business model into sharp focus.

Try designing a brochure for your entire practice, and one for each niche.

1. Start with a blank 8 1/2 X 11 sheet of paper, placed the long way in front of you.

2. Fold the right side 1/3 to the left, fold the left side over the right. You should end with a tri-fold of 3 equal sized sections, the top page opening from the right.

3. Label the top page 'COVER,' write 'Graphic,' and 'Headline: Problem Statement or Solution Statement.'

4. Open the top page and label the page on the other side 'PAGE 1.' This is the page on the left when you open the brochure. Write 'Facts about problem' and 'Solutions/Benefits/Promises.'

5. Label the page to the right 'BACK/FOLDOVER.' This is the page that opens to the right, and is on

the back when opened. Write 'Top Tips' and 'Educational.'

6. Open the Foldover page and label the middle section PAGE 2, and the right section PAGE 3.

7. On Page 2, write 'Service Delivery System' (services, programs, and features) and 'Contact info.'

8. On page 3, write 'Top-Testimonials,' 'Middle— Calls To Action/Offers/Invitations,' and 'Bottom-Short bio and photo.'

9. Fold up the brochure and turn it over. Label 'BACK' and write 'Mailer'

Adapt the above to your preferences and then FILL IN THE BLANKS!

Seven Easy Steps to a Basic Web Site

I am writing this article assuming you don't have a web site yet, and know absolutely nothing about them. Hopefully there will be some gems for web-savvy readers as well.

External marketing, meaning getting new clients from your web site, or selling products and services on your web site, is beyond the scope of this article.

At its most elemental, a web site is an on-line brochure for internal marketing to your existing leads, a way for prospective clients to learn more about you.

Just as most helping professionals have a business card and brochure, most should have at least a basic web site. Most prospective clients have internet access and would check your web site if you referred them. Your web site can provide information about you and your services that inform and attract your prospective clients, helping them make the leap from first learning about you to hiring you.

Here are some suggestions for getting started:

1. GET A DOMAIN NAME

I strongly suggest you decide upon a domain name for your web site and e-mail that expresses what you do. Even if you don't intend to have a web site, *Barbara@GreatCoach.com* is far more effective and professional than *Barb123@aol.com*

If you are not tech savvy, I recommend *http://www.verio.com* for searching and purchasing your domain name. The cost is $19.00 per year. Verio is a large, well-established internet service provider, and their customer service is very good.

At $8.95 per year, *http://www.godaddy.com* is a very affordable domain name registrar.

You can also use your own name as your domain name, either with a 'dot com' address as in Coach@DavidSteele.com or with the new 'dot name' domain as in David@Steele.name. I have multiple domain names, and use *David@Steele.name* as my personal e-mail address, and *www.David.Steele.name* for my personal web site address.

2. GET A WEB HOST

Option A: DO-IT-YOURSELF

There are excellent and cost effective do-it-yourself web hosts. If you are starting out and need to watch your cash flow, this is a good way to go. Check out:

http://www.homestead.com
http://www.tripod.lycos.com
http://geocities.yahoo.com/home
http://www.angelfire.lycos.com

You can get an advertisement-free web site with e-mail and user-friendly do-it-yourself web building tools for $4.95 per month. Make sure to choose the option that will let you use your domain name as the web site address.

Option B: IF YOU USE A WEBMASTER

If you plan to hire a web master, you should still design your own content and choose a web host. For inexpensive web hosting:

---

http://www.godaddy.com
http://www.fastwebserver.com
http://www.behosting.com

Option C: USING YOUR CURRENT ISP

You use your Internet Service Provider to dial into the internet, and to send and receive e-mail. Many ISPs provide web hosting, and it may even be an included feature of your account that you are not using. Before spending money on a web host, make sure you don't already have one with your current ISP.

3. LINK YOUR DOMAIN NAME TO YOUR WEB HOST

Once you sign up with a web host, you will get the info you need to link your domain name to your web host. If you can't figure out how to do this yourself, call tech support. This is where your choice of vendor makes a difference beyond price—Verio tech support will hold your hand and do it for you, and I've had tremendous trouble even finding the contact information for tech support for some internet service providers.

4. CONFIGURE YOUR E-MAIL SOFTWARE TO USE YOUR NEW DOMAIN NAME

You will need to change your e-mail settings to show your domain name on the 'From' and 'Reply To' fields, as well as download and send your e-mail from your new web host's server. In Outlook Express, you click Tools> Accounts> Add, then follow the wizard's instructions. Your web host will provide the settings and passwords needed—make sure to *print out and keep* the document from them with this information.

5. DESIGN CONTENT

Even if using a web master, you need to decide what you want on your web site and provide them the content. They can give you ideas about appearance, navigation, and features, but you need to take charge of the content. Be sure to check out other like professionals' web sites to get ideas for yours.

Just like a brochure, you want to have information about you and your services, but I suggest you also provide articles and content of value for your prospective clients. What do you want them to know that would encourage them to hire you? The more value you provide on your web site, the better your results will be. If you have written some articles, this is a great place to showcase your work. You can obtain content from other web sites and authors, just be sure to request their permission.

TIPS:

➢ Make your web pages interesting with graphics and/or pictures. Put your picture on your web site, casual and friendly, regardless of your resistance to doing so

➢ You can find lots of clip art at *http://www.clip-art-gallery.com* or *http://www.clipart.com*

➢ Need a logo? Create your own for free at *http://www.webgfx.ch/startwebgfx.html*

6. INSTALL YOUR 'CALLS TO ACTION'

In your e-mail signature line, as well as your web site, you need at least one, preferably more, calls to action.

This can include subscribing to your newsletter, taking an on-line quiz, contacting you for a complementary session, informing their friends, etc.

Some need only be an invitation of text; others, like a quiz or subscription box involve advanced web features you may need help with.

For more info, see *'Get Results With A Call To Action'* in "Best Practice Building Tips"

7. INTEGRATE WITH YOUR INTERNAL MARKETING SYSTEM

Your web site should refer to your newsletter and your newsletter should refer to your web site. Your outgoing voicemail greeting and e-mail signature can refer to both.

Create a system for engaging your prospective clients and building your relationship with them using the pieces you have put in place.

Remember that 80% of sales are made with 5 or more contacts; your web site can be an integral part of how you build your relationship with your prospective clients in the process of helping them decide to make the wise decision to work with you.

Over time, you can add content and more advanced features to your web site that generate more traffic, provide more value, and even generates revenue. Hopefully this article will help you get started.

Ten Revenue Streams for Helping Professionals

I believe we all have talents and gifts, and can achieve great things by following our passion.

Recently I compiled a list of how I generate income, and was astounded at how far I have come since my days as a traditional Marriage And Family Therapist in private practice, counting TEN revenue streams in addition to seeing clients 1:1.

If I can do it, so can you. Here is a list of my ten revenue streams, and I invite you to consider how you can follow your passion and add each one to your business:

1. TANGIBLE, STRUCTURED PROGRAMS

The public wants tangible benefits and solutions.

I packaged my approach to helping singles and couples have successful relationships into my 'Relationship Success For Singles' program and 'Partners In Life' for couples, which proved to be effective in attracting clients. See *http://www.LifePartnerQuest.com*

In addition, I developed '5 Day e-Programs' for singles and couples, a 'Practice Building Intensive' for helping professionals, and I'm just warming up! ;-)

2. GROUP PROGRAMS

Classes, teleclasses, workshops, and my favorite—the

'Coaching Team' (a model of group coaching that I developed). Classes are popular and appeal to our potential clients because they offer useful, practical information, are time limited, at an affordable price. Besides generating income, class participants are our best prospective 1:1 clients.

3. TRAINING OTHER PROFESSIONALS

Having developed my own approach for coaching singles and couples, I offer training for others who want to expand their practice and skills by learning useful, proven concepts, methods, and practice tools, and not recreate the wheel. See *http://www.RelationshipCoachingInstitute.com*

4. LICENSING PROGRAMS

Having developed effective structured programs for my niche, other professionals can license the use of these programs.

5. WORKBOOKS AND MANUALS

Clients and other professionals can purchase hard copies or download from my web site.

6. MENTOR COACHING

My favorite—I really enjoy helping other professionals design and build their practices. My experience and track record in building my own give me credibility to mentor others.

7. PROFESSIONAL COMMUNITIES

I created a community of coaches in my niche in Relationship Coaching Institute, as well as a community of clients in my niche in LifePartnerQuest-Silicon Valley. People need and benefit from community participation and support, and if they receive value and tangible benefits, they are willing to pay for membership.

8. E-PROGRAMS

I developed an e-version of my practice-building program, and e-programs for singles and couples.

9. AFFILIATE PROGRAMS

Members of my affiliate program receive a percentage of any sales referred to my web site. In addition, I refer to selected organizations/businesses whose products I support and believe in, some of whom have affiliate programs, and I receive a commission.

10. CO-BRANDING

Partnering with like and complementary organizations and businesses to offer our services under their name. This is an easy way for them to add to their revenue streams, typically without cost or effort on their part. For example, partnering with a local singles organization to offer our classes under their name to their members and customers.

HOW MANY WOULD YOU LIKE TO ADD TO YOUR PRACTICE?

I would love to help you transform your dreams for your practice into reality, and generate income from 10 different directions. Contact me for Mentor Coaching if this appeals to you.

———

Using Auto-Responders to Market Your Practice

Auto-responders provide immediate responses by e-mail to your clients and potential clients 24/7, and are valuable marketing and practice management tools.

An auto-responder is a system that automatically sends your message once someone sends an e-mail to a certain address. Over time, I have come to increasingly appreciate auto-responders and the possibilities for using them in my business.

Here is how I currently use auto-responders. Hopefully, you will be inspired to increase their use in your practice as well.

1. 5 DAY E-PROGRAMS

I recently launched my first 5 Day E-program for singles: *'HOW TO FIND THE LOVE OF YOUR LIFE.'* I plan other 5 Day E-programs for singles, couples, and professionals.

An 'e-program' is a program in which you participate by e-mail. In my 5 Day E-Programs an e-mail is sent once a day for five days. Each e-mail consists of useful information, suggestions, actions to take, marketing-related invitations, links for more information, etc.

For ideas, and to see how this works, check out *'How To Find The Love Of Your Life,'* by sending a blank e-mail to *lpq5dayprogram@getresponse.com*

To develop your own 5 Day Program:

Step 1: Choose one of your niches

Step 2: List your top 5 tips addressing a compelling problem, solution, or goal for people in that niche

Step 3: Explain each tip, give some context

Step 4: Include some suggestions and actions to take

Step 5: Include links to your web site for more info

Step 6: Include a variety of invitations to engage you

Step 7: Paste above on an auto-responder
(see 'Where To Get Auto-Responders' below)

2. NEWSLETTERS

I currently have 3 newsletters, all of which are set up on auto-responders. This only works with an auto-responder that has a broadcasting feature independent of the programmed messages.

There are several advantages to using an auto-responder for newsletters:

1. Low cost, without advertising (Free to $6.00 per month, rather than $10-$30.00 per month for some broadcast services)

2. Automated subscribe, unsubscribe, and management of bad addresses—included at no extra cost

3. My favorite—you can easily set it up so that new

---

subscribers immediately receive your current
month's newsletter

To check out my newsletters and see how this works, you
can send a blank e-mail to any of the addresses below:

SINGLES—*LPQ-7513@autocontactor.com*
COUPLES—*LPQ-9327@autocontactor.com*
PROFESSIONALS—*LPQ-7514@autocontactor.com*

If you do, you will receive two e-mails immediately—a
'Welcome' e-mail and the current month's newsletter. The
'unsubscribe' link is at the bottom of every e-mail.

3. 'OUT OF OFFICE' AUTO REPLIES

This is probably the most common use of auto-responders, and most ISP's provide this feature.

If you are off-line for more than a couple of days (vacation, business trip, hospitalization, etc) it is good service to
your clients and prospects to set up an auto-responder to let
them know, AND you can include marketing related invitations.

For example:

'Thank you for contacting me. I am currently on
vacation and will respond to your message when I
return on May 15th. If you need assistance before
then, please contact _____.

For cutting edge information about relationships
and my programs for singles and couples, please
subscribe to my FREE monthly newsletter by visiting
http://lifepartnerquest.com/subscribe.htm

Some folks set up an auto-reply that responds immediately to every e-mail, such as 'Thank you for contacting me, I will be in touch shortly.' While well intentioned, I wouldn't recommend this, unless you set up a special e-mail address for prospects in which a prompt response is important, such as Inquiry@YourDomain.com.

4. FOR MORE INFORMATION . . .

To increase the interactivity of your web site, you can use auto-responders to send specialized information by e-mail instead of providing all the content on your web site. Examples would be your rates/policies, your e-book, detailed recommendations, results of an on-line assessment, etc. This makes your web site more interactive and engaging to your prospective clients, which is more effective in building your relationship with them.

One major advantage of doing this is to capture the respondent's e-mail address for future follow-up. Most visitors to your web site will not e-mail or call you without a compelling reason, and this is a way to increase the effectiveness of your web site for generating new leads/prospects. This is permission marketing; each respondent is 'opting in' as interested in what you offer, giving you permission to contact them, and if they don't wish to be contacted further, they can always 'opt-out' by clicking the link at the bottom of each e-mail.

Then, you can program follow-up e-mails in your auto-responder to keep in touch with your prospects. These e-mails can have more information and invitations that may interest them. While you can do this with a newsletter, this method results in more targeted leads, and you can reach prospects that may not subscribe to your newsletter.

Believe it or not, some folks are reluctant to commit to subscribing to a newsletter, but are more open to requesting specific information by auto-responder, and the immediate response is very attractive, even exciting!

For example, visitors to my web site for singles are invited to take my RELATIONSHIP READINESS QUIZ at *http://lifepartnerquest.com/single/quiz/* which asks for their e-mail address before taking it, and their results and follow up are e-mailed by auto-responder. Do you think participants might be counting the seconds until they get their results?

5. E-PUBLISHING

It is a common marketing practice to publish e-books and provide them as complementary downloads, usually in PDF format. I have discovered that many tech-challenged folks have trouble with PDF, and many people don't wish to read a book on their computer.

Would you download and read all the articles in this *Best Practice Tips* series on your computer? Some would, some wouldn't. Having this series of articles on auto-responder gives you the choice.

As long as you are providing free information (presumably to help market yourself, as I am), you might as well make it as widely accessible and as easily readable as possible. By setting up your chapters on an auto-responder, you can send them out daily or weekly (you set the schedule), you can revise them at any time, and you can include timely marketing invitations.

An example of using an auto-responder for e-publishing is the excerpts of my upcoming book for singles, *'Conscious Dating: Finding The Love Of Your Life In Today's World.'* To receive 18 daily excerpts, one from each chapter, send a blank e-mail to *ConsciousDating@getresponse.com*

WHERE TO GET AUTO-RESPONDERS

1. *First, check your current ISP,* web host, or shopping cart provider. You may already have this feature available to you.

2. *GETRESPONSE.COM* is very reliable, easy to use, full of features, cost effective, and allows for independent broadcasting. I decided to use them for my 5 Day Programs and Conscious Dating book excerpts. The free version includes ads, which I would not recommend. I pay under $6.00 per month for each of these two auto-responders by paying for 3 years in advance. A very important feature is that I can program the sending address with my e-mail address, so each e-mail appears to be coming from me.

   Check them out at *http://www.getresponse.com/index/44541*

3. *FREEAUTOBOT.COM* has the advantage of being free, supposedly without advertisements, however each e-mail DOES have an advertisement—for FreeAutobot.com! Scroll down to check it out.

   They don't have the features of GetResponse.com, such as broadcasting, and I would rather not have the word 'Free' in the sending address, as it is not as professional. However, if you want a free auto-responder, their ads are less obvious than the free version of Getresponse.com.

   Check them out at *http://freeautobot.com/*

---

4. *SHOPPING CART:* My newsletters and auto-responders related to purchases on my web site are on a system included with my shopping cart account on 1Shoppingcart.com. While not costing me extra and being full of features, I have found their system unreliable for sending out scheduled broadcasts of a series, such as this series, my book excerpts and 5 Day Programs. However, I highly recommend them as being a cost effective, easy-to-use, full-featured shopping cart provider with good customer service, and they work well for my newsletters and other non-serial auto-responders.

Check them out at *http://www.1shoppingcart.com/app/default.asp?pr=1&id=16864*

EASY WAYS TO MARKET YOUR AUTO-RESPONDERS

1. *YOUR NEWSLETTER:* I have a regular 'Invitations' section at the bottom of each newsletter inviting readers to get more information from my web site and auto-responders.

2. *YOUR WEB SITE:* I have an invitation to sign up for my free 5 Day Program Singles on every page related to singles at www.LifePartnerQuest.com

3. *YOUR E-MAIL SIGNATURE:* If you are interested in marketing your practice, having a free and compelling invitation in your e-mail signature is very effective and costs nothing.

I know many practitioners who are not yet doing this, mostly because they haven't figured out how. If this is you, *DO THIS NOW!*

For MS Outlook Express, click Tools >Options >Signatures. You can design your signature in another document, and paste it in.

Here is my e-mail signature:

David Steele, MA, LMFT, CLC * Relationship and Mentor Coach
David@Steele.name * *http://www.David.Steele.name*

Check out my Free E-Programs! (just send blank e-mail to the address below)

5 DAY E-PROGRAM FOR SINGLES—> *LPQ5DayProgram@getresponse.com*
CONSCIOUS DATING—> *ConsciousDating@getresponse.com*

Free Relationship Coaching training / Free relationship newsletter
http://www.RelationshipCoachingInstitute.com

---

4. *'PLEASE SHARE WITH INTERESTED FRIENDS AND FAMILY':* People forward cool stuff they discover on the internet because it is an easy way to keep in touch with, and help, people they care about. You can help this process along by suggesting it directly whenever and wherever you can.

CONCLUSION: We know that 80% of sales are made with 5 or more contacts. Auto-responders are a great way to easily provide value, increase your # of contacts, and build your relationship with your prospective clients.

Auto-responders are easy to use, inexpensive (even free!), and very effective marketing and practice management tools. They work for you 24 hours a day, and are well worth the time to set them up.

Converting Prospects to Customers

Most prospective clients don't know you, and are not motivated to hire you for an intangible service. They want solutions, answers, something tangible.

To make the intangible, tangible, you can have brochures, business cards, a web site, a newsletter, even a book, but that is not enough for most prospects who think of your service as an expensive, open-ended relationship, where there is no guaranteed outcome.

Even though most of your prospects might agree with the value of what you do, they STILL hesitate. How can you convert these prospects to customers?

Many helping professionals rely on a "sample session" or "free initial consultation." In my experience, takers usually have already decided to work with you, so it may unnecessary for them, and won't reach prospects that are interested but not ready to commit to making an appointment, even if free.

The enrollment activity/mindset I recommend is the 'Enrollment Conversation' where you invite them to talk over the telephone (or in-person if that is the context in which you meet them) about what they want and help them real time. They get an EXPERIENCE of working with you *before* committing to anything.

We need to remember that even though we believe our service is wonderful, in most cases prospects will be more interested in what they can get out of the service, the benefit to them, then you or your service itself, and won't commit to an appointment (even if free) until they are convinced.

The goal here is creating a customer where none existed before, which is challenging, but VERY rewarding as most of our potential clients fall into this category.

Think of a car salesman (easy metaphor, but not a close analogy!) trying to sell a car to a wealthy woman that doesn't even really like cars; he can't convince her of what a great deal it is, how much integrity he has and that she can't go wrong by buying from him, and he can't sell her on the features (airbags, ALB, MPG, etc), if that is not important to her.

He finds out what is important to her first by asking 'What do you want?' ('I just want something that gets me where I want to go without hassle and doesn't aggravate my arthritis riding in it') and speaks to that; 'This car will get you where you want to go, comfortably, and won't give you any trouble'.

For that woman, or any inquiry, my approach would start by asking what the prospect is seeking (some version of 'What do you want?'), then speak to that.

Prospects want answers, solutions, and you could simply give them the answers they seek, but you know that achieving their goal is not as simple as that, so you speak to what they want, ask more questions, share tidbits that demonstrate your expertise and the value of your services, and help them learn something important about themselves—providing real value in a 5-10 minute conversation.

In the enrollment conversation you ask questions and want your prospect to:

1. Touch their passion for what they want (by talking about it)

2. Experience their frustration about what has not been working (by telling stories)

3. WOW them with new info/technology they had no idea existed

4. Learn something new about themselves so they really experience the value of your services and that 'you don't know what you don't know'

5. WANT to talk with you MORE!

Closing Questions To The Enrollment Conversation

1. Has this been helpful to you?
2. Would you like to continue this conversation sometime?
3. When would be good for you?
4. (Optional) Do you know anyone else that can benefit from my services?

➢ **TIP**: I recommend following the above steps and waiting for the prospect to ask "How much do you charge?", "How does this work?", or similar question.

When they ask about your fees they are seriously considering your services. Bringing up your fees before they have decided to work with you can sabotage their decision-making process.

If they don't bring fees up during the Enrollment Conversation, they almost always will do so at the beginning of your first appointment. If not, you can find an opportunity to do so early in the first appointment when discussing how you will be working together. In the beginning, the goal for unsure prospects is to focus more on helping them and the benefits of working together, than on what it costs and being paid.

Very few people will expect you to work for free, but focusing on spending the money before they are comfortable doing so will sabotage enrollment. If they do not bring it up at the beginning of the first session, be careful not to give away your services—continue asking questions and gently lead them to discussing how to work together.

Ten Ways to Make Your Services Tangible

One of the challenges in marketing an intangible service counseling, coaching, and many helping professions, is that potential clients need something tangible to relate to in order to make the leap of faith needed that your services are worth their time and money.

You already understand and buy into your service, your potential clients don't. Imagine that your prospective client is highly skeptical and reacts to you like a 'get rich quick' scheme-

'OK, let me get this straight; you want me to pay you hundreds of dollars and you are somehow going to help me be happy and successful—yeah right!'

Your marketing must educate them about your services and the benefits to them in a convincing manner by making what you do highly tangible.

Here are some ideas for you:

1. **'KEEPERS'**; such as bookmarks that I hand out to singles with the '10 Principles Of Conscious Dating' on them. A 'keeper' is any object useful to your client that they might want to 'keep'.

Keepers such as pens, buttons, key rings, etc, that simply advertise are not as effective. I like the idea of using business cards as keepers by having an inspirational or informational message on the back, such as a tips list.

2. **AUDIOTAPES**; my enrollment rate skyrocketed after I developed a 'Finding The Love Of Your Life AND The Life That You Love' audiotape for singles. It can be a big expense, about $2000.00 and up to get started, but they have a long shelf life, they get recycled as recipients pass them on to friends, and once the audiotape is made, handing it out is not much more expensive than most brochures.

Try taping yourself next time you give a presentation, workshop, or class, and see if you can tweak the content for a promotional audiotape. You can also produce audiotapes of your work to sell—this is quite easy to do.

3. **COLLATERAL MATERIALS**; are the traditional way of making the intangible tangible. These are items such as logos, brochures, business cards, stationary, fictitious business names, etc.

Your collateral materials present your image to the world, and can be expensive to do well, but if done right, you won't have to do it again, and will serve you effectively for a long time. See "Basic Brochure Design" in this book.

➤ **Resource**: Check out *www.VistaPrint.com* for FREE business cards and affordable stationary, labels, postcards, etc. They make it easy to design your own on-line.

4. **PREVIEWS**; a bite-sized piece such as the 'enrollment conversation'. This is giving your prospective client a tangible experience of your service.

———

Many helping practitioners attempt to use this by offering a 'free initial consultation', however, my experience is that this only works when the prospective client is pretty much already sold. The challenge is to design previews that appeal to your target audience. *Assessments* are great previews, and allow you to learn about the prospective client to specifically reinforce how your service can benefit them. For singles I offer a "Relationship Readiness Quiz" that you can check out at *http://lifepartnerquest.com/single/quiz/*

5. **CLOTHING**; can be a very cost-effective means of getting your message and image to your prospective clients. T-shirts and caps are inexpensive and easy. We wear high quality polo shirts embroidered with our logo at singles events, classes, conferences, etc. This makes our image and organizational affiliation very tangible.

You could have polo shirts made up to wear yourself to present a professional image, or you can have t-shirts made up to give away or sell with a catchy message that promotes you.

6. **INFORMATION**; is one of the best ways of making your intangible service tangible to your prospective clients, using mediums such as handouts, web sites, books, newsletters, e-zines, recordings, self tests, etc.

People love information, especially if it is free, especially if they think they will benefit from it. Use language such as 'How to.', Learn to.', 'Top 5 Tips For.', etc.

If people like your information, they will be attracted to you. For example, even though the '12 Dating Traps' (see *http://lifepartnerquest.com/single/trap.htm*) has very little to do with my singles coaching program, the information is interesting and compelling enough that singles become interested in our program when they learn about them.

7. **FOCUSING ON BENEFITS**; many marketers make the mistake of focusing on things that are important to them, and not what is important to their prospective clients.

It's fine that you are affordable, convenient, experienced, etc, all of which are 'features'. Your prospective clients need to know what they can 'get' from working with you, how will it benefit them, how will their life be different, how will they get what they want?

8. **PACKAGING**; design a packaged service and market it. For example, instead of marketing 'relationship readiness' coaching for singles, we packaged it into the 'Relationship Success Training For Singles Program' (see *http://www.lifepartnerquest.com/single/finding.htm*), which makes it more tangible. When a pre-committed or pre-marital couple contacts me, I describe my 'Partners In Life Program' of specific activities and deliverables for a specific price. Most couples continue after the four sessions, but the 'package' helps convince them to get started. (See *http://www.Partners-In-Life.com*)

9. **DIFFERENTIATION**; what do you want to be known for? How are you different from other practitioners? Why should a client hire YOU? This involves making yourself tangible by clearly defining yourself as a professional, and your ideal

---

client, then figuring out how to position yourself so your ideal client is attracted to you and can pick you out of a crowd.

10. **REPETITION**; is the most effective way of building a relationship with your prospective clients and making you tangible to them. Keeping yourself and/or your name in front of them over and over.

I do this with e-mail newsletters, e-programs, autoresponders, special announcements, etc. Whatever your specialty, you can come up with different reasons to get in front of your prospective clients over and over; for example, using holidays as a reason to have a special event or service, such as 'How to have a blast on Valentines day', 'Self care during the Christmas season', 'Find a date for New Years', etc.

Marketing Effectively with Presentations

Giving presentations is the second most effective marketing strategy for helping professionals (#1 is getting referrals from clients). Most successful practitioners regularly give presentations.

There are two primary ways to give presentations; organizing your own event, or presenting to a gathering organized by others.

Organizing your own events is the best means of promoting your services, as you can control all the variables, and results in more highly qualified leads.

There are also two primary modalities for giving presentations; in person, and over the telephone in conference calls or teleclasses. Soon, internet radio, chats, and streaming video will become more common ways to present to an audience.

Below are 10 ways to maximize your marketing effectiveness when giving presentations.

1. RULE #1—GET CONTACT INFO!

If your event is free, the price of admission should be that people give their contact info.

Have everyone register before entering on a sign-in sheet with at least their name, e-mail address, and telephone #. Have several clipboards so it doesn't hold things up. If a teleclass, use a registration system where you give the bridge # to participants only after you have their e-mail address. If you are presenting in a venue that doesn't have a built-in means of collecting contact info, get creative!

2. PROVIDE MULTIPLE OPPORTUNITIES TO 'OPT-IN'

For example:

(1) On the *registration form*, add an 'opt-in' line for them to check 'Yes! Please subscribe me to your informative newsletter' or similar offer.

(2) Have a *sign up sheet* for a promotion, such as a free assessment, seminar, teleclass, e-program, etc, with a prominent sign, somewhere in the room.

(3) Have a checklist of 'Please contact me about____' on the *event evaluation*, etc.

(4) Have a *drawing* where they sign up or drop a business card in a box to win a book, tape, service, etc.

(5) The signature line of every *e-mail* should have an invitation to subscribe to your newsletter, contact you about a service, etc.

3. FOLLOW UP YOUR LEADS

If you followed Rule #1, almost everyone attending should be a lead, as well as people that contacted you that they were interested but couldn't make it.

In the day or so after the event, contact them all in some way. You could send them a thank you note, sample newsletter (e-mail or snail mail), invitation to your next event, a 'call to action' to contact you by a certain date for a free service, call them to connect/invite/ask for feedback, etc.

The attendees that 'opted in' gave you their permission to contact them, and the ones that didn't will most likely not object to a one-time, respectful (non-pushy) contact.

4. FOLLOW UP YOUR EVENT!

Leverage your time, effort, and expense of putting on an event by planning follow-up events. Plan them a year in advance—weekly, monthly, quarterly, etc. Announce the dates and topics to everyone that attends or expresses interest, and ask them to tell their friends. Include events organized by others in which you will be presenting.

➤ *NEVER leave without the audience knowing the next opportunity to catch your act.*

5. CREATE A SYSTEM

Leverage your time, effort, and expenses by planning the details of how to market and implement your events, how to generate and follow up leads, how to convert prospects to clients, who your target audience is and what services/products they want/need that you will offer them, how to promote word of mouth (the most effective marketing strategy!), how you will get everything done and who will help you, etc.

➤ *Do everything that you can to make these decisions once, in advance, to maximize your efforts and minimize costly trial and error and disorganization that will sabotage your success.*

6. PROMOTE ENGAGEMENT

Use name tags, enlist volunteers to free you so you can personally greet everyone as they come in, provide light refreshments during breaks, organize a pre-event mixer and/ or group, use ice-breakers, make your presentation interactive, break them into small groups, *do all that you can to involve/engage everyone present.*

7. GET FEEDBACK

At the end, pass out or e-mail a short evaluation form and ask attendees to fill it out. Ask how they liked the presentation, what topics they would like to hear in the future, and most importantly, have a short checklist beginning with *'Please contact me about'* and include your services, products, and a place for them to put their name and telephone #.

8. PROVIDE TAKE-AWAYS

Such as handouts from your presentation, an audiotape, pen, bookmark, fliers, announcements, schedules, newsletters, article reprints, brochures, business cards, etc, all with your contact info prominently displayed.

Even better, organize all these in a folder, envelope, or bag to pass out to attendees. By e-mail these can be notes from your presentation, additional information, and links to articles and resources (if too much text for the body of an e-mail, convert to PDF using Adobe Acrobat so all recipients will be able to read them).

9. FOLLOW-UP CONTACTS

The following statistics are from marketing guru Fred Raley:

2% of sales are made on the 1st contact
3% of sales are made on the 2nd contact
5% of sales are made on the 3rd contact
10% of sales are made on the 4th contact
80% of sales are made on the 5th-12th contact

This means you need a way to stay in touch with your leads through newsletters, announcements, special offers, future events, seasonal promotions, etc. It is incredibly easier and more effective to market internally than externally, so *your efforts mining your existing leads have the highest chances for success.* DON'T DROP THE BALL!

10. BUILD YOUR CONTACT DATABASE

Success is a numbers game, and you will be much more successful with a list of 2,000 qualified prospects than not.

Your goal should be to steadily build your contact list name-by-name, contact-by-contact. If you have an announcement or newsletter list (and you should), ask recipients to forward to their friends. Look for opportunities everywhere you go to identify prospects and exchange contact information, and to seek opportunities to present, especially in groups and settings where your ideal client is likely to be.

How to Handle 'I Can't Afford it Right Now'

PROBLEM: Often we talk to potential clients who express an interest in our services, only to hear them say that they 'would like to, but cannot afford it right now.'

QUESTION: How can we shift prospects from scarcity mentality to abundance mentality, from potential clients to clients?

> **SOLUTION #1**: Educate them about the Law of Attraction. (Wherever you place your attention, that is what will come to you.).
>
> Once they understand the concept, ask them:
>
> > A. If this is what you are thinking (e.g., I can't afford it), what do you think will come to you?
> >
> > B. How can you attract abundance?
> >
> > C. How can you attract what you want?
>
> **SOLUTION #2**: Discuss turning crisis into opportunity.

When people lose their job, they are often in a crisis mode. This is a prime time for people in such circumstances to re-define their lives. Help them see the opportunities open to them at this time and how your services will help them go forward with their life.

SOLUTION #3: Do an 'Abundance Exercise.'

Help them get beyond their scarcity mindset by asking them to think about what abundance they have in their lives. Help them see that they already have abundance. Ask them what they are grateful for, what their strengths, assets, and opportunities are.

SOLUTION #4: Use a box metaphor for a paradigm shift from scarcity to abundance.

At the present they are in the scarcity box. When you are in a box you can't see that there are other boxes out there.

Ask if they are willing to switch boxes to the abundance box. What would that look like? What opportunities are open to them in this new box that wasn't in the old box? What is the payoff for them staying in the scarcity box, and what is the cost?

SOLUTION #5: Turn 'I can't!' into 'How can I?'

We often tell ourselves (and others) 'I can't . . . I can't afford it. I can't find the time. I can't find anyone right for me. Ask them to write out all the things they 'can't' do. Then ask them to change each of these to 'How can I?' Suggest that they ask their friends to help them figure out how they can do these things. Barbara Sher *www.barbarasher.com* talks about this in her book 'Wishcraft.'

———

SOLUTION #6: Assess whether the person is ready for change by either asking them directly ('I wonder if you are ready for change?') or indirectly by listening to them and asking other questions. If your assessment is that they are not ready, don't waste your time trying to convince them.

Seven Steps of Guerilla Marketing

By Jill Lublin, author of 'Guerrilla Publicity'

So you've started your own business and you're ready to let the world know! Now it's time to add public relations to your list of entrepreneurial skills.

Public relations is human relations and a critical aspect of growing your business. Everything you say and do is part of your PR campaign. It is the image you project every day to everyone you meet. PR can be a primary way to grow your business and become known without major expense.

There are seven basic steps to mounting your campaign:

STEP 1: Figure out how to express WHO you are and WHAT you do in the most succinct and INTER-ESTING way possible.

There may situations such as networking functions where you have only 30 seconds to introduce yourself and make that all important first impression. Spend as much time as necessary practicing your 'intro' until it truly flows in a positive, strong, and confident manner.

STEP 2: Determine your "OOH-AAH" factor; the 'story' about you.

It's important to understand why you are news from the

media's perspective and how your products help people or your service gives value and benefit.

Once you know your 'ooh-ahh' factor, you can begin to create materials, which will tailor your story to the specific media, whose attention you wish to gain.

STEP 3: DEFINE your audience and create a media list.

Your list will be determined by the nature of your product or service, whether you are a local, national or international company and on which markets you are focusing your growth. If you are a 'local' trying to build a business in your community, then you will focus on local media. It's important to familiarize yourself with all the media you contact and to make preliminary phone calls to get the appropriate name for directing your release or media kit.

STEP 4: Put together a PRESS RELEASE, a simple 3-4-paragraph one-page document that tells your story clearly.

It must be unique to grab media attention FAST. The first paragraph must contain the 'catch' phrase to grab them quickly. It should contain the Who, What, When, Where, Why, and How of your story, and begin with the city and state of origination.

Techniques for grabbing attention include giving a statistic that shows that their audience needs this information, which makes it relevant to current events or business news. The second paragraph might consist of a quick biography or additional information and the third should contain a quote from the highest source you can find. Sometimes the press will only use the first paragraph so it must contain all the relevant information.

The press release should be done on your letterhead. On the top left hand column it should say FOR IMMEDIATE RELEASE. The upper right should show the CONTACT and give your name and phone number. Be absolutely sure it is 100% accurate in terms of grammar, facts, punctuation, spelling, and names.

STEP 5: Create a MEDIA KIT, which will include a copy of your press release(s) as well as other information.

This is used to create interest for the press to do a full story or having you appear on a TV or radio show. It should also include a company background piece or brochure, a pricing sheet, any press clippings (reproduced on your stationary) and any other public relations materials. Grabbing attention is imperative so packaging is critical. It involves the careful selection of eye-catching colors for the folder as well as the contents. Quality says a lot so don't skimp.

STEP 6: FOLLOW THROUGH!

Presumably you have created your media list and have the appropriate names with (correct spelling) and titles. Now comes the most critical part, the follow up! The phone may not ring. It is up to you to make the calls. Start by saying, 'hello, my name is 'and start your pitch within 10 seconds Remember your hook' and tell them in 30 seconds or less why you are the news. A good rule of thumb on follow up calls is within one week for national, within three to four days for local/regional or if email, with a day or two. You might want to create a one-page synopsis to use as a guide when you call which should include who you are, why you are news, and how your product or service benefits people and gives value.

STEP 7: *SEVEN REMINDERS to help you create powerful publicity 365 days a year.* If you follow these tips, you will be well on your way to capturing the media's attention!

1. Make PERSONAL CONTACTS as often as possible.

2. Always carry your BUSINESS CARD and materials.

3. Know what is SPECIAL about you and get the word out using the media.

4. KNOW THE MEDIA you are pitching—always watch or listen to a show before you are on it.

5. BE PREPARED for interviews. They might just call you before you call them.

6. BE CONSISTENT with your image and make sure all your materials reflect the image you desire to project.

7. PARTICIPATE in social and civic activities and help others get business by networking.

Jill Lublin is an internationally acclaimed speaker on public relations and marketing. As CEO of the PR strategic consulting firm Promising Promotion and founder of GoodNews Media, Inc. Jill hosts the nationally syndicated radio show 'Do the Dream. Author of two audio tapes, and a workbook, Jill's newest book Guerrilla Publicity (Adams Media) is part of the best selling Jay Conrad Levinson Guerrilla Marketing series. She can be reached at (415) 883~5455, email to jill@planetlink.com or at *www.promisingpromotion.com*

Writing Winning Headlines

American Writers & Artists Institute
www.awaionline.com

To make a headline work, you have to make it specific enough to be intriguing but vague enough to provoke curiosity. The purpose of the headline is not to sell the prospect — it is to capture his attention and engage him in the selling process.

Following are nine frequently used types of headlines. Pick up just about any successful sales letter and you'll likely run into one of them:

1. 'HOW TO'

This is the most popular and most effective of the archetypes. A good place to start with any assignment. Many headlines aren't nearly as compelling if you remove the 'how to.' These two words act as a command for your prospect to carry out.

EXAMPLES:
* 'How to End Your Money Worries Forever'
* 'How to Win Friends and Influence People'

2. THE BIG BENEFIT

This headline puts your biggest, most compelling benefit right up front.

EXAMPLES:

---

* 'Earn $5,000 Next Weekend Without Leaving Your EasyBoy Recliner'
* 'Pay Zero Taxes Next Year!'
* 'Lose 40 Pounds in 7 Days Without Dieting!'

3. NEWS STYLE

This refers to a headline that sounds like editorial copy. To make it work well, it is helpful to have some legitimate news to talk about. You might, for example, be promoting a new product. Or you might uncover some new facts related to an old product.

EXAMPLES:

* 'New Natural Hormone Promises to End Cancer Without Chemotherapy'
* 'Dentists Are Outraged — New Book Reveals How to Get Free Dental Care!'
* 'Skinny School Teacher Gains 15 Pounds of Muscle WithMiracle Meal'

4. THE ANXIETY HEADLINE

Scare your prospect into paying attention. Give him a problem and the hope of solving it.

EXAMPLES:

* 'What Will You Do When Your Personal Assets Are Seized to Satisfy a Judgment Against Your Corporation?'
* 'Do You Make These Mistakes in English?'

5. PERSONAL REVELATION

Offer an interesting admission about a topic your prospect should be interested in.

123

EXAMPLES:
* 'They Thought I Was Crazy to Ship Maine Lobsters As Far As 1,800 Miles From the Ocean.'
* 'The Lazy Man's Way to Riches'
* 'They Laughed When I Sat Down to Play the Piano . . . But When I Started to Play'

6. THE QUESTION

Ask a question that implies a promise, a benefit, or a solution. (But make absolutely sure you know what your prospect's answer will be.)

EXAMPLES:
* 'Why Is Your Dog Eating Dirt?'
* 'Tired of Making Your Boss Rich?'
* 'Do You Close the Bathroom Door When No One Is Home?'

7. THE TESTIMONIAL

If you've done your research, and have a convincing case history, this can be one of the easiest headlines to write . . . and very powerful.

EXAMPLES:
* 'I Gambled with 3 Cents and Won $35,850 in 2 Years.'
* ' I Couldn't Believe My Eyes When I Tore Open the Envelope!'

8. THE STORY

Everyone likes to read a good story.

EXAMPLES:
* 'The Insult that Made a Man Out of Tim Riley.'
* 'The Greatest Story Ever Told'

9. THE GUARANTEE

When you are pretty sure your prospect wants your product — and you want to give him a reason to choose yours over the competition — this type of headline can be very effective.

EXAMPLES:
* 'Play Guitar in 7 Days or Your Money Back!'
* 'The Most Comfortable Shoes You've Ever Worn, or Your Money Back!'

One way you can make your headline writing go faster and better is to write a half dozen or so headlines for each of these nine types. Six times nine gives you 54 heads to choose from. Not a bad start.

© 2001 American Writers & Artists Institute
Visit *www.awaionline.com* for **FREE** biweekly newsletter

Top 5 Writing Mistakes

As a private practice professional it is important to communicate effectively with your prospects and clients. In composing text for your brochure, web site, announcements, newsletter, etc, here are my top five writing mistakes to avoid:

1. SPELLING ERRORS

Use your spell checker! Proofread everything you send at least 3 times for items the spell checker misses. Ideally, have someone with good writing skills proofread for you as well.

2. GRAMMATICAL ERRORS

If we want to build trust and credibility, grammar is as important as spelling. Even the best educated confuse 'it's' and 'its,' and has trouble remembering to put the punctuation inside quotation marks (which are my most recurring errors!). There are grammar checking books and software, or you can go on-line for free at *http://www.grammarstation.com/GC.html*

3. USE OF CLICHES

A turn-off. If you aren't sure if a phrase is a cliche or not, a fun site to visit is *http://www.clichesite.com/ index.asp*

4. USE OF JARGON

Another turn-off. You lose your reader (and

possibly the prospect/client) when you use language your prospects and clients don't understand.

Remember, you are writing for THEM, not for YOU! Define your terms . . . even better, use plain language so you don't need to do so!

5. TOO MUCH TEXT

Edit everything you write to its most concise form. Most good writers spend much more time editing their writing down than actually writing!

For web sites, use lots of bullets and outlined points. For e-mail text especially, such as e-mail newsletters and correspondence, break up text into short paragraphs of a sentence or two.

I suggest reviewing the web sites, newsletters, announcements, brochures, etc of the leaders in your field and identify:

A. What they do well that you would like to emulate

B. What they don't do very well that you could improve upon

BONUS WRITING TIP:

When writing marketing copy for your prospects, emphasize BENEFITS, BENEFITS,BENEFITS! Address what your prospects and clients care about and want, not what you think is important.

'Don't tell me about your grass seed; tell me about my lawn.'

Get Results with a 'Call to Action"

A *'Call To Action'* is an invitation for your prospective clients to actively engage you in some way—directly or indirectly.

Most prospective clients, even if they are very interested in working with you, often need a way to build a relationship with you in bite-sized pieces to work up to engaging your services.

Effective marketing will ALWAYS include a *SPECIFIC, EASY, TARGETED, COMPELLING,* and usually *FREE,* call to action.

Everything you send out can and should include a call to action; e-mails (in the signature line), web site, flyers, business card, advertising, announcements, newsletters, even the outgoing greeting of your voicemail system.

> ➤ **KEY QUESTION**: What can you invite your prospective clients to do, what can you offer them, that they would be likely to act upon, that would build your relationship with them?

Common calls to action for coaches include offering a free coaching session, contacting you for more information, subscribing to your newsletter, and visiting your web site.

They are OK, but there are so many interesting alternatives . . .

SOME IDEAS:

Free assessment
Free teleclass or in-person seminar
Contest
Polls, brainstorming (best movies, books, vacation
   spots, dates, etc)
Free E-book
Free E-program
Free audiotape or web audio recording
Free "How-To" articles, tips lists by auto responder
Significant discount for fast response, early
   registration
"Ask The Coach" feature on web site and/or
   newsletter
Free participation in pilot program
Participate in research project
Scheduled instant messaging (IM) chat hours
Scheduled telephone call-in hours
Tip Of The Week

For example, if you are a relationship coach targeting couples, in your e-mail signature line and newsletter you could put the following:

'Want BETTER COMMUNICATION with your partner? E-mail (auto-responder) for your copy of my 'Top 5 Communication Tips For Couples' '

AND/OR-

"FREE ONLINE COACHING! Join me for "LoveCoach Chat" on AIM Tuesdays and Thursdays 7-9pm. Screen name "LoveCoach." E-mail (auto-responder) if you would like information about downloading and using AIM."

Of course, along with the auto-responder e-mail you would send a warm letter inviting them to take further action to engage you . . . .

➢ NOW, HERE IS A CALL TO ACTION FOR YOU!

Build Your Dream Practice!

Join my 90 Day Practice Building Intensive program-www.BuildingYourIdealPractice.com
Individual Practice Development Coaching also available. Interested? Contact me today!

Effortless E-Mail Marketing

There are two no-brainers if you use e-mail to communicate and are serious about your practice:

1. GET A DOMAIN NAME
Choose a registrar such as *http://www.godaddy.com* (8.95 per year), *http://www.fastwebserver.com* ($15.00 per year) or *http://www.verio.com/* ($19.00 per year with top notch customer service) and use their search box to find a domain name that appeals to you.

Why?

1. If you change your ISP you won't have to change your e-mail address with everyone you know

2. It provides a professional image. Which looks better to you-*barb123@aol.com* or *CoachBarb@GreatRelationships.com*??

In addition, I would NEVER use a free e-mail service such as Yahoo or Hotmail for professional correspondence.
Then, your e-mail address will market for you every time you send an e-mail.
Effortless . . .
You do NOT need a web site to get a domain name—

you can use it for e-mail alone. Then, when you are ready to put up a web site, you will have your domain all ready to go.

I suggest you create a name that speaks to your mission, purpose, and vision.

2. USE AN E-MAIL SIGNATURE

This is very easy to do once you figure out how. Almost all e-mail software will allow you to append a signature, and if it won't (or until you figure out how) you can paste one in.

For Microsoft Outlook Express, click Tools >Options >Signatures. You can design your signature in another document, and paste it in.

For ideas, check out the signature line of e-mails you receive. Here is mine:

David Steele, MA, LMFT, CLC * Relationship and Mentor Coach
David@Steele.name *http://www.David.Steele.name*

Check out my Free E-Programs! (just send blank e-mail to the address below)

5 DAY E-PROGRAM FOR SINGLES—> *LPQ5DayProgram@getresponse.com*
CONSCIOUS DATING—> *ConsciousDating@getresponse.com*
BEST PRACTICE BUILDING TIPS—> *lpq-18920@autocontactor.com*

Free Relationship Coaching training / Free relationship newsletter
http://www.RelationshipCoachingInstitute.com

A good e-mail signature is inviting and includes a compelling 'call to action,' such as signing up for your newsletter, getting a free e-book, taking an on-line assessment, etc.

Since you send e-mail anyway, this is effortless. In addition, when your e-mail gets forwarded, others will see it as well.

Top 5 Ways to Handle E-mail Effectively

As you increasingly use e-mail to market and correspond with prospects and clients, participate in on-line communities, keep in touch with friends and family, etc, you may need to take some steps to handle your e-mail effectively. *These are my top five recommendations:*

1. GET ANTI-VIRUS PROTECTION

Without anti-virus protection, you *WILL* eventually experience a crash of your computer and lose all the data that you have not backed up. This is a frustrating and costly experience that you can easily avoid.

RECOMMENDATION: if you do not have anti-virus protection, IMMEDIATELY go to *http://www.mcafee.com/myapps/vso/default.asp?* and sign up for McAfee's VirusScan Online for $29.95 per year. This is CHEAP and effective insurance. You will be glad you did.

2. DO NOT OPEN ATTACHMENTS!

Got your attention? Good. Let's expand on that to say 'Do not open attachments unless you are sure about them,' because most viruses are delivered as attachments to e-mails and can be very seductive in tempting you to open them, including using the e-mail address of someone you know.

How to be sure that an attachment is OK to open?

Look for these 3 things:

A. FAMILIAR SENDER
If you know the sender, you STILL must be careful and follow the steps in B and C below. NEVER open an attachment from an unfamiliar sender—delete immediately!

B. EXPECT THE ATTACHMENT
In today's world, most of your fellow computer users know not to open unexpected attachments, and shouldn't expect you to do so as well.

If the attachment is from a familiar sender, but unexpected, *DO NOT OPEN IT!*
Viruses can get sent unknowingly from anyone's address book—even yours!
Send them an e-mail and ask them if they sent you an attachment, and if so, 'what' and 'why?'

C. FAMILIAR FORMAT
Look at the file extension of the attachment, which are the letters after the dot following the name of the file. If in a familiar format, such at JPEG (graphic/pictures), TXT, DOC, etc, you are probably safe—IF you know the sender AND expect the attachment. *NEVER* open attachments with EXE, which is a program that will execute itself immediately when you open it.

3. USE FOLDERS LIBERALLY
Keep your inbox as empty as possible by creating

---

folders for all the kinds of e-mail you receive. If you don't have a place for an e-mail and you don't want to delete it, *create a folder for it!* You can use folders for projects, people, organizations, niches, newsletters, possible newsletter items, etc.

Once your e-mail is organized into folders, you can easily locate them for future reference, and can more easily back them up onto a disk.

4. MANAGE YOUR TIME

Do not allow your e-mail to rule your life. Decide when, how often, and how long you will check and work on your e-mail. It is tempting to be reactive and check your e-mail multiple times per day, answering everything that comes in immediately. Unless you are at your desk all day and work on your computer for a living, this is not a good idea if you want to have a life.

5. DELETE SPAM

This might sound like an obviously simple statement, but many don't follow it.

Spam is unsolicited promotional e-mail, and a fact of life that we can't avoid. No spam filter will screen out all spam. If you try to follow their instructions to remove yourself from their lists, you will receive even *more*, because you have confirmed for them that your e-mail address is valid and that you read unsolicited e-mail. There are some tricks to minimize spam that are beyond the scope of this article, and won't eliminate spam anyway, so there is no substitute for using your 'delete' button.

For some users, is not unusual to receive 200+ e-mails per day, including 100+ spam e-mails per day. When downloading a day's e-mail, it takes less than a minute or two to visually scan your inbox for spam and delete them. Like junk mail from the Post Office, don't feel like you have to read each one, or try to get removed from their list. Your life will be far simpler if you just delete them quickly and move on.

How to Get and Use Testimonials

Testimonials are crucial to marketing your services. They help answer common objections, build your credibility, and stimulate your prospects into action.

Good testimonials are believable and compelling when they are *specific, concise,* and *dramatic.*

A very effective way to get good testimonials is to interview your clients. Yes, actually *interview them*!

INTERVIEW QUESTIONS FOR GETTING EFFECTIVE TESTIMONIALS

1. What made you decide to work with me?
2. What do you appreciate most about working with me?
3. What do you most value about how I work with you?
4. What pivotal moment or event in our working together made a big difference for you?
5. How is your life different as a result of our working together?
6. Would you recommend me to others? What would you tell them?

Transcribe the interview then edit their comments down to the fewest words possible.

Then, share the result with your client and ask them for their permission to use it with their name. Testimonials are far more credible if you are able to quote the source by name.

WHERE TO USE TESTIMONIALS

-Web site
-Brochure
-Announcements, fliers, and sales letters
-Newsletter
-Books and e-books

EXAMPLE OF A GOOD TESTIMONIAL

Take a look at the testimonials at
www.BuildingYourIdealPractice.com

Notice the five testimonials at the top:
"Practical solutions that really work"
"rich in content"
"complete road map"
"simple, yet powerful"
"working less, making more"

Concise? Dramatic? Specific?
Realize they are highly edited from actual testimonials that are longer.
For example, **"working less, making more"** came from the following testimonial that appears further down on the page:

> "*How To Build Your Ideal Practice In 90 Days* has been a great help in building and transforming my practice. After being in private practice for 12 years, I finally found someone to teach me about the business of it all.
>
> The clincher, however, is that it all works!! I am working less, making more, but most of all, I am hav-

ing more fun and feeling more in control of what I do . . . .

Thanks David!!"

—Ken Donaldson, M.A., L.M.H.C., Seminole, FL

Of course, the above version is edited as well! As you read it, ending with Ken's name, city, and state, do you see how effective it is to be able to use his name?

Try reading it and cover up the name . . . see the difference?

As you scroll down the page at *www.BuildingYourIdealPractice.com* and skim the testimonials, do you see how they help overcome common objections, build credibility, and stimulate prospects into action?

Conclusion

Good testimonials don't expire, they can be used again and again for a long time. It is absolutely worth overcoming your resistance and taking the time and trouble to collect them. When you have them-

USE THEM! Help your prospects become comfortable with you by sharing what others have experienced about you.

III
APPENDIX

Invitations

1. **Join my 90-Day Practice Building Intensive**
   Why be alone? Join a supportive community of professionals like you for mutual support and networking. Featuring weekly conference calls led by David Steele and an e-mail discussion list. For more information go to
   http://www.BuildingYourIdealPractice.com

2. **Sign up for your FREE 30 Minute consultation with David Steele**
   Stuck? Overwhelmed? Need creative ideas for your personal brand? Get the support you need! To arrange your free telephone consult, e-mail *david@steele.name*

3. **To receive FREE e-mail updates and bonuses**
   Send a blank e-mail to *LPQ-23067@autocontactor.com*

CLIENT TRACKING FORM

Name	(N)ew/ (P)rev.	Appt. Kept✔	Source Code	Reason for Visit	Fees Collected	Follow-up /

Source Codes:

A= Professional referral   F = _____

B=Client referral   G = _____

C= Web site   H = _____

D= Newsletter   I= _____

E = _____ J = _____

One Year Practice Building Planning Calendar

Date Prepared:	Months:												
Internal Strategies													
External Strategies													

1. Insert months across top, starting with current month   2. List strategies   3. Plan start date for each strategy

145

Top Seven Recommended Resources

In addition to the many resources mentioned above, I have personal experience with the following resources and recommend them highly with complete confidence

- **Accepting Credit Cards:** *Practice Pay Solutions*
  Best rates and service for private practitioners
  http://www.profcs.com/app/aftrack.asp?AFID=22872

- **Shopping Cart System For Your Web Site:**
  1Shoppingcart.com
  Full featured, affordable, and user-friendly
  http://www.profcs.com/app/aftrack.asp?AFID=22872

- **Coaching Resource:** *Coachville*
  FREE! Training, referrals, innovative programs such as "Passive Income," "100 Day Full Practice e-Program," and much more. www.Coachville.com

- **E-Mail Auto Responder:** *Getresponse.com*
  Reliable, user-friendly, free option, great for newsletters, e-programs, etc
  http://www.getresponse.com/index/44541

- **E-book and e-program covers:** *Killer Covers*
  Vaughan Davidson is very creative, affordable, and has high integrity

  http://hop.clickbank.net/?dasteele/vdavidson

> **Public Relations leads and contacts:** *PR Leads*
> Dan Janal offers an effective and affordable way to
> access local and national media
> *http://www.prleads.com/*

> **Incorporating your business:** *Active Filings*
> Easy, affordable, reliable, excellent service
> *http://www.activefilings.com/cgi-bin/ya/*
> *click.pl?id=dasteele*

Resource Index

The following is an index of resources listed in this book, as well as a few selected others.

ACT!—Contact management software—http://www.act.com/

ActiveFilings.com – easy, affordable on-line business incorporation service

Adobe Acrobat Reader – download the latest version FREE—http://www.adobe.com/products/acrobat/readstep2.html

American Writers & Artists Institute – Free newsletter, resources for effective writing—http://www.awaionline.com/

Conscious Dating e-Program – Free chapter excerpts of David Steele's book for singles

GoDaddy.com – Inexpensive web hosting and domain name registration—http://www.godaddy.com/

LifePartnerQuest.com – Relationship information for singles and couples—http://www.lifepartnerquest.com/

LPQ Newsletter For Singles Or Couples—http://lifepartnerquest.com/subscribe.htm

LPQ On-line Quiz For Singles—http://lifepartnerquest.com/single/quiz/

LPQ 5 Day e-Program For Singles—mailto:lpq5dayprogram@getresponse.com

McAfee.com – Anti-virus protection—http://www.mcafee.com/myapps/vso/default.asp?

Practice Building Intensive – 90 Day program FREE with the purchase of this book—http://www.relationshipcoachinginstitute.com/practicebuilding.htm

Practice Development Coaching – FREE 30 minute consult with

David Steele with the purchase of this book—http://www.david.steele.name/

PromisingPromotion.com – PR programs by Jill Lublin, author of "Guerrilla Publicity"

QuickBase – Free on-line database system by Intuit—http://www.quickbase.com/

RelationshipCoachingInstitute.com – Relationship Coaching training, certification, and marketing support for helping professionals

Relationship Coaching Institute Newsletter—http://www.relationshipcoachinginstitute.com/forms/subscribe.htm

Verio.com – Web hosting and domain registration with good customer service

VistaPrint.com – Free business cards, on-line design and ordering

Webgfx.com – Free logo design and web site tools

Webmaster – Ken Douglass is my webmaster. He is affordable, reliable, and creative—http://www.kwebs.biz/

Yahoo Groups – Free listserv, calendar, e-mail, database, file storage/sharing, etc—http://www.yahoogroups.com/

Web Hosting—FREE:
http://www.homestead.com
http://www.tripod.lycos.com
http://geocities.yahoo.com/home
http://www.angelfire.lycos.com

Web Hosting and domain name registration—affordable:
http://www.fastwebserver.com
http://www.behosting.com
GoDaddy.com

About The Author

David Steele, MA

- Licensed Marriage and Family Therapist
- Certified Life Coach
- Founder and CEO of LifePartnerQuest and Relationship Coaching Institute

What I do

As a *Practice Development Coach*, I coach helping professionals to design and build the business of your dreams!

As a *Relationship Coach*, I help singles and couples to have successful Life Partnerships.

As a *Mentor Coach*, I train helping professionals to apply coaching skills and tools in helping their clients have successful relationships.

As the *Founder and CEO* of *LifePartnerQuest* and *Relationship Coaching Institute* I develop effective relationship coaching tools, concepts, and programs, and promote relationship coaching to the public and helping professionals as the method of choice for helping singles and couples get what they want from their life and relationships.

My Mission

My mission is to vastly improve the success rate of committed relationships in our community by:

Coaching singles and couples to have successful Life Partnerships

Developing and applying a Coaching model of helping singles and couples have successful relationships

Mentoring and training coaches and therapists to be successful Relationship Coaches

Collaborating with other helping professionals in establishing the profession of Relationship Coaching as a visible, effective, credible, preferred choice for helping people have successful relationships

Professional

Over 25 years experience in counseling profession

Over 15 years full time private practice specializing in relationships—California Licensed Marriage and Family Therapist #21897

Pioneer in development and application of five-stage coaching model for helping singles and couples have successful relationships (Readiness, Attraction, Pre-commitment, Coupling, Bliss) www.LifePartnerQuest.com

Founder, CEO, and creative force behind *LifePartnerQuest* for singles and couples, and *Relationship Coaching Institute* for training helping professionals; innovative, progressive relationship coaching organizations that are re-inventing the practice and delivery of relationship support services

Author of *Conscious Dating: Finding The Love Of Your Life In Today's World.* www.ConsciousDating.com

Author of the audio program *Finding The Love Of Your Life—AND-The Life That You Love,* available FREE at *http://lifepartnerquest.com/audio/*

Author of the pioneering *Relationship Success Training For Singles Program* for helping singles to "find the love of your life and the life that you love."

Author of *Partners In Life,* an innovative coaching program for pre-committed and pre-marital couples.

Author of *Practice Building Intensive* and *Build Your Ideal Practice In 90 Days* for assisting helping professionals to design and build your ideal practice. For info go to *www.BuildingYourIdealPractice.com*

Editor of *Relationship Coaching News,* a monthly e-zine for helping professionals featuring innovative information about relationship coaching and practice development. http://lifepartnerquest.com/subscribe.htm

Personal

I am the devoted father of young twin boys and a teen-age daughter, and am in a committed relationship with my life partner Maggie.

LifePartnerQuest is the result of my own journey in being passionate about healthy, successful relationships and being twice divorced, which has taught me much about what works and what doesn't work in relationships that I have been able to bring to my professional work and benefit others. Having a successful marriage and family are still my top priorities!

I enjoy hiking, backpacking, biking, diving, sailing, family activities, and am an avid do-it-yourselfer around the house!

Coaching Style

I am very direct, creative, goal-oriented, interactive, positive, intuitive, supportive and nonjudgmental.

I stay focused on your goals and agenda and emphasize teaching the information and skills you need to be successful.

I delight in helping my clients reach beyond what they thought realistic or possible!

Selected client comments

I am so very grateful for your *creative and inspirational coaching.* Thank you for your *focus, expertise and kindness,* I feel *supported and energized*—an exciting combination that is helping me *move clearly forward*—without feeling overwhelmed! — L. H.

In a few short weeks, you helped me gain *MUCH clarity.* Your questions steer me to think about things that haven't crossed my mind before. You offer *VERY practical suggestions* while giving me plenty of room to explore the options I want. When we are on the calls, I have your full attention and it feels like I have a partner! — F.M.

David Steele is dynamic, energetic, and informative; he *offers much more value* than I expected.—C.M.

Working with David Steele as my coach has been a Godsend. From our very first session, he has been able to help me *clarify my goals, establish my priorities, put wings on my vision* and most importantly of all, he expects me to *take action.*

This isn't just a "feel-good" experience, (although it does give me joy and hope), but it's a *practical hands-on,* let's roll-up-our-sleeves-and-get-this-thing-done relationship that makes it so worthwhile.—J.H.

Other areas of coaching expertise

> Entrepreneurs
> PracticeDevelopment/Marketing
> Blended Families
> Men's Issues
> Workplace Issues
> Career and Life Coaching
> Single Parenting
> Divorce Recovery

Contact info

> E-mail: *David@Steele.name*

> Web sites:
> *www.LifePartnerQuest.com*
> *www.ConsciousDating.com*
> *www.David.Steele.name*
> *www.RelationshipCoachingInstitute.com*
> *www.BuildingYourIdealPractice.com*

Mailing address:
P.O. Box 111783
Campbell, CA 95011

Telephone: 408-261-3332 ext. 11
Fax: 408-369-9164

Printed in the United States
28360LVS00002B/46-57